Keeping it in the community

An evaluation of the use of mediation in disputes between neighbours

GW00382549

Linda Mulcahy

with

Lee Summerfield

Copyright in the typographical arrangement and design in vested in The Stationery Office Limited. Application for reproduction should be made in writing in the first instance to the Copyright Unit, Her Majesty's Stationery Office, St Clements House, 2–16 Colegate, Norwich NR3 1BQ.

The information contained in this publication is believed to be correct at the time of manufacture. Whilst care has been taken to ensure that the information is accurate, the publisher can accept no responsibility for any errors or ommissions or for the changes to the details given. Every effort has been made to trace copyright holders and to obtain permission for the use of copyright material. The publishers will gladly receive any information enabling them to rectify any errors or ommissions in subsequent editions.

A CIP catalogue record for this book is available from the British Library
A Library of Congress CIP catalogue record has been applied for

First published 2001

ISBN 0 11 702553 4

Printed in the United Kingdom by The Stationery Office
TJ3879 C6 4/01

The Nuffield Foundation is a charitable trust established by Lord Nuffield. Its widest charitable object is "the advancement of social well-being". The Foundation has long had an interest in socio-legal issues and has a special programme of grant making in "Access to Justice". The Foundation has supported this project to stimulate public discussion and policy development. The views expressed are, however, those of the authors and not necessarily of the Foundation.

About the authors

Linda Mulcahy LL.B, LL.M, Ph.D is Anniversary Reader in Law at Birkbeck College, University of London. She has previously held posts at the Universities of Bristol, Oxford, South Bank, North London and the Law Commission. She has published widely on disputes and has recently conducted an evaluation of the NHS medical negligence mediation pilot scheme. Linda is chair of the Socio-Legal Studies Association and a research consultant at the Public Law Project.

Lee Summerfield B.Sc, M.A. is a Research Fellow at the National Audit Office and at the time of the study was a Research Fellow at the University of North London. He was previously employed at South Bank University where he worked with Linda Mulcahy on an empirical study of complaints across the public sector. Lee has also worked on an evaluation of peer mediation in schools.

Table of Contents

About the authors   **iii**

List of Tables, Figures and Boxes   **xi**

Acknowledgements   **xiii**

**Chapter 1:
Introduction**   **1**

Increasing interest in neighbour disputes and mediation	1
The growth and promise of community mediation	4
Shared ideas	7
The core features of practice	9
The aims and methods of the research	10
The organisation of this report	10

**Chapter 2:
A critique of informalism and community mediation 17**

Introduction	17
Healing community rifts?	18
Reducing state control?	19
Reinforcing existing inequalities?	20
The value of peace?	22
Conclusion	23

Chapter 3:
About Southwark Mediation Centre   25

Introduction   25
    Location and staffing   25
The work of the Centre   27
    The Housing project   28
    Environmental Services project   28
    The Five Estates project   28
    Other projects   29
Changes at the Centre – funding and visibility   29
    Towards a professional service?   31
Conclusion   32

Chapter 4:
Management of disputes by housing officers   35

How many disputes reach the council?   35
To what is mediation an alternative?   39
The role of the housing officer   41
    Stages in the dispute-handling process   42
    1. Understanding the issues in dispute   42
    2. Formal letter   43
    3. Court action   44
Referring cases to mediation   45
Mediator views of referrals   49
Conclusion   50

Chapter 5:
Disputes and their causes – Towards a politicisation of grievances   53

Number of disputes handled by the mediation agency   53

The dynamics of the dispute   55

Who gets involved in disputes?   57

    What do disputants complain about?   60

    External causes of neighhourhood disputes   62

Conclusion   64

Chapter 6:
The processing of disputes at Southwark Mediation Centre   67

Introduction   67

    What happens to disputes referred to SMC?   67

    The unseen workload   71

Conclusion   74

Chapter 7:
A description of the mediation process   77

Introduction   77

The mediation process   78

Shuttle mediation   78

What happens on home visits?   80

    a. Preliminaries   81

    b. Exploration of issues   82

    c. Seeking options for the future   83

Face-to-face mediation   84

Control of process   86

Techniques used during shuttle and face-to-face mediation   87

     Facilitating communication   87

     The use of empathy   89

Conclusion   90

Chapter 8:
The many roles of mediators   93

Introduction   93

A flexible approach to process and neutrality   93

     Mediation ambassador   96

     Translator   97

     Peacemaker   99

     Counsellor   102

     Adviser   103

     Message bearer   104

Conclusion   106

Chapter 9:
The costs of neighbour disputes   109

Introduction   109

Methods   109

SMC funding and organisational costs   112

     SMC overhead costs   112

Time spent by mediators on general and specific tasks   114

     What are the costs associated with mediation activities?   116

What is the total cost of individual cases?   119

Assessing the wider costs of neighbour disputes   120

     Agency costs   120

     Costs to the individual and society   120

Conclusion   121

Chapter 10:
Conclusion   **123**

Introduction   123

The 'problem' of neighbour disputes   124

Putting the research in context   125

The shadow of the law   126

A promising development   127

Reconstructing disputes   130

In closing …   131

References   **133**

List of Tables, Figures and Boxes

Tables

1.1	Summary of methods	12
1.2	Summary of additional methods	14
4.1	Noise complaints recorded by Southwark noise team from April-September 1999	38
5.1	Gendered dynamics of disputes referred to mediation agency	57
5.2	Classifications of disputing parties	58
5.3	Allegations made in 91 cases in which the agency made contact with both the complainant and the respondent	60
6.1	Type and frequency of contact with complainants and respondents	72
9.1	Sources of data, purpose of analysis and problems experienced	111
9.2	Sources of funding	112
9.3	Southwark Mediation Centre expenditure	113
9.4	Breakdown of general mediator tasks by individual mediators in hours	115
9.5	Breakdown of specific mediator tasks by individual mediators in hours	116
9.6	Breakdown of mediator tasks in an average month	117
9.7	Case costs and cost per employee 1997/98 (Housing, ES and Five Estates)	119

Figures

4.1	Formal complaints are just the tip of a disputes iceberg	37
4.2	Routes of resolution	40
4.3	Number of referrals over 12-month period by neighbourhood office	46
5.1	New cases by year and project	55
5.2	Number of close cases referred on by SMC	59
6.1	Closure of cases 1995-9 Housing and ES	69
6.2	Processes used to manage neigbourhood disputes over one year	70
6.3	Level of activity with complainant	73
6.4	Level of activity with respondent	74

7.1	Process stages of home visits	81
7.2	Arrangement of the parties at a face-to-face mediation session	85
9.1	Total annual costs per mediator by task	118

Boxes

4.1	Views of mediation	48
5.1	The generation gap	54
5.2	The patter of tiny feet	56
5.3	Misuse of overflow pipe	56
5.4	The deaf old lady	58
5.5	Dirty linen in public	61
5.6	Rites of passage	61
5.7	Examples of noise allegations	62
7.1	Description of role and establishing credibility	78
7.2	Information flow	88
8.1	The superiority of mediation to law	96
8.2	Accentuating the positive	100
8.3	Conveying the positive	101
8.4	Mediating between the individual and state	105
8.5	Managing expectations	105

Acknowledgements

The authors would like to express their thanks to a number of people who have made significant contributions to this report. First and foremost our thanks go to the staff at Southwark Mediation Centre for the time they have devoted to the project. They have been generous and good humoured collaborators. We have also benefited from the insights provided by Guy Valentine, housing officers and residents in the borough. We would like to make clear our debt to Sharon Witherspoon at the Nuffield Foundation who has shown patience and given support throughout the project. Without the grant made by the Nuffield Foundation the research would not have been possible. As always, Marie Selwood has provided a high level of technical support. Stuart Scott and Heulwen Summerfield have provided essential assistance in conducting and transcribing interviews.

Chapter 1: Introduction

1.1   This report evaluates the use of community mediation in the resolution of disputes between neighbours in one London borough. The issue is one of increasing importance as policy makers stress the value of keeping disputes out of the courts and users of formal grievance procedures continue to express concern about the inability of such systems to provide satisfactory outcomes. Debate between practitioners and academic researchers about the value of mediation has come to something of a stalemate. Proponents of mediation often make ambitious claims about the value of the process while critics have been vociferous in their claims that the practice of mediation does not live up to the bold claims made by such evangelists. This report is one of the first major evaluations of the use of community mediation in the UK and suggests a number of ways in which debate about the value of mediation can be progressed. It steers a difficult course between the optimism of many champions of mediation and the pessimism of early critics and raises the question of whether community mediation can be successful in ways not anticipated by proponents and opponents to date.

1.2   The research on which this report draws was generously funded by the Nuffield Foundation. This chapter explains why the research is important. It is in three sections. The first section considers the reasons why policy makers and academics are increasingly turning their attention to the issue of how neighbourhood disputes are best managed. The second section discusses the growth and promise of community mediation and the philosophies underpinning the claims of community mediators that this form of resolution provides a more successful approach to conflict within communities than more formalised redress systems managed by state officials. The final section describes the methods adopted by the research team and the way in which the rest of the report is organised.

Increasing interest in neighbour disputes and mediation

1.3   A significant proportion of the population has experience of neighbour disputes and it is clear that they can have an intensive and long-lasting impact on the quality of peoples' lives. Many disputing neighbours choose to resolve their problems without seeking the help of a third party. Others put up with their sense of grievance (Genn 1999). For those who seek assistance in trying to sort out a problem with a neighbour, the ease with which they can access state agencies for advice and help is an important test of the extent to which the state is serving the needs of the citizenry in facilitating redress of grievances.[1]

1.4   Research on disputes is also important for other reasons. Caplan (1995) asserts that the study of disputes leads straight to key issues for social scientists - norms and ideology, power, rhetoric and oratory, personhood and agency, morality, meaning and interpretation. Disputes dominate many discussions of social interaction because of what they reveal about communities and relationships in the modern state. Although they seem to be out-of-the-ordinary events, they nevertheless mobilise support systems, highlight social cleavages and are argued in terms of general morality (Colson 1995). Trubek (1980-1) has contended that analysing disputes offers the possibility of greater insights into social relations and conflict because they can be used to understand the wider social world in which they are embedded. It allows us not only to see social relations in action but also to understand cultural systems and the relationship between social structure, indigenous ordering and formal law.

1.5   The implications of inappropriate handling of neighbour disputes are enormous. This is especially the case for those living in social housing in the inner city. These disputes do much to reveal power relations in the modern state and the tensions implicit in living in disadvantaged, over-crowded, poorly maintained social housing. Public sector tenants are amongst the most socially disadvantaged in society and are effectively locked into their environment, since moving to another area is rarely an option. On-going hostile relations with neighbours can make the home environment seem intolerable and can lead to lack of sleep, depression, assaults and sick leave. Neighbour disputes also have a radiating effect on the local population. They can affect levels of tension and the general sense of well-being and stability within communities.

1.6   Those living in the inner city experience a shortage of housing which means that residents from different generations and with different lifestyles are often housed close by each other. It has also been claimed that the 'right-to-buy' policy of the last Conservative administration led to an increasingly mixed population and less tolerance on the part of home owners about environmental noise and conditions (Liebmann 1997). The introduction of a care in the community policy for mental health has also led to many more vulnerable people residing in the community, often inadequately supported. Many more people in the inner cities are at home during the day and night because of the higher than average incidence of illness, old age and unemployment and, as a result, are more exposed to their neighbours' activities. Finally, much noise-making equipment is a great deal more powerful than was ever anticipated when high-density social housing was constructed in the post-war years.

1.7   Another reason for heightened awareness of neighbourhood disputes has been that they appear to be on the increase. While conflict between neighbours is confined to a relatively small minority of householders, when extrapolated to the UK population the numbers involved are likely to be very large. Dignan and colleagues (1996) have reported that the number of neighbour nuisance complaints reported each year to local authority housing and environmental health service departments could be upward of 250,000, about two-thirds of which are likely to be noise related. Environmental health officers have reported that the number of noise-related disputes has risen from 1412 per million population in 1981 to 6903 in 1995/6. Liebmann (1996) contends that the number of noise complaints per million of the population increased 20 per cent between 1991/2 and 1992/3. Coupled with concerns about the inefficiency of the courts and the expense of litigation, these arguments have provided compelling incentives for policy makers to embrace mediation which is generally, although inaccurately, perceived as saving costs (see Mulcahy *et al.* 2000; Dignan *et al.* 1996). Although the Chartered Institute of Environmental Health Officers has contended that the rise in noise disputes may be attributed to an increased propensity to complain rather than an increase in noise levels (Chartered Institute of Housing 2000).

1.8   Neighbour disputes make significant calls on public sector resources. Dignan *et al.* (1996) reported that local authorities have found their officers spending increasing and disproportionate amounts of time on these problems. Aldbourne Associates (1993) estimated that housing officers spent about a fifth of their time dealing with disputes between neighbours and Southwark Mediation Centre (SMC) has estimated that the London Borough of Southwark alone is currently spending some one million pounds a year on neighbour disputes. In addition, a number of other public sector agencies such as the police, environmental health and social services may get involved in attempting to resolve such problems.

1.9   There have been many criticisms of the ways in which disputes between neighbours are being handled by local authority landlords. Concern has come from many quarters including policy makers, the voluntary sector, media, ombudsmen, consumer groups and academics (see, for example, Karn *et al.* 1993; McCarthy *et al.* 1992; Tebay *et al.* 1986). Criticisms have focused on the inappropriateness of the courts intervening in the healing of rifts between those in a long-term relationship and the lack of skills amongst local authority employees in dealing with these types of conflict.

1.10 One response to such concerns has been the policy trend towards encouraging the use of more informal methods of dispute resolution. It has been frequently argued that the need for neighbourhood mediation has also increased as the number of disputes between neighbours has risen (Haslam 1996). Lord Woolf's review of the civil justice system in the mid-1990s heralded a 'shifting down' of cases from the formal adjudicatory system to more informal mechanisms for resolution (Lord Chancellor's Department 1996). Lord Woolf made a special investigation of housing litigation and after discussing actions for disrepair and possession, judicial review and the Local Government ombudsman, he moved on to discuss the potential offered by community mediation:

> *There is a limited but important role for other forms of alternative dispute resolution in housing cases. Mediation, in particular, is widely recognised as being the most effective way of resolving many disputes between neighbours, although it is clearly not appropriate in cases of serious nuisance or anti-social behaviour. A minority of local authorities already provide mediation services, and it would be helpful if these could be extended. (p.220)*

1.11   Moreover, in his interim report (1996a) he argued:

> *[Mediation agencies] have made a considerable contribution to the resolution of disputes, resulting in a significant saving to the court system. Almost without exception the bodies which provide these mediation services are underfunded. This is not in the interests of their clients or of the Court Service. I recommend that they are funded more appropriately. I would very much hope that in any review of legal aid the needs of bodies of this nature would be taken into account. In many situations, they provide the only way in which the citizen can obtain access to justice, and in any event they may offer a better and less confrontational way of dealing with disputes between neighbours, where a continuing relationship is often important.(p.141)*

1.12   His comments reflect a much wider interest in using mediation for the resolution of disputes and recent years have seen the launch of a number of government-funded research projects to evaluate the effectiveness of mediation as an alternative to the courts (see, for example, Genn 1998; Mulcahy *et al.* 2000). Whilst none of these pilot schemes involve community disputes, state sanctioning of community mediation in the Woolf report suggests that, contrary to popular belief, such initiatives are not always community driven.

The growth and promise of community mediation

1.13   Mediation has been heralded as one of the most vital and far reaching procedural reforms of our time (Delgado *et al.* 1985). Its proponents claim it offers speedy, accessible, flexible justice for the common person. It is argued that those who are threatened or intimidated by formal courts may be willing to bring their problems to a less formal arena. Neighbour disputes display many of the characteristics which have been associated with successful mediation initiatives (Brown and Marriot 1993; Murray, Rau and Sherman 1989). Most notably they are inter-personal, polycentric and the parties have an on-going relationship. These are features of disputes that other dispute resolution mechanisms - which are adversarial, individualised and rights-based - are not well-equipped to handle.

1.14 The first community mediation centres were set up in the early 1980s in London and there has been a significant increase in their number since then. Many of the early centres were largely dependent on the vision of particular people or groups, including professionals such as probation workers and psychologists and religious groups such as the Anglican clergy and Quakers (Liebmann 1997). In the United States, community mediation has become the most pervasive form of mediation (Murray *et al.* 1989) and the number of centres has also grown rapidly there (Delgado 1985). In the UK, the majority of community mediation schemes are concerned with neighbourhood conflict although many direct their attention to victim offender work and to working with schools (Liebmann 1997). Billinghurst (1996) has reported that, of the 110 mediation organisations which are members of Mediation UK, the only national umbrella group for such organisations, 68 per cent are concerned with community and neighbourhood mediation as opposed to victim offender work and conflict resolution in schools. In addition to offering mediation, these centres may also be involved in mediation training, liaising with community groups and giving advice about conflict management. Community mediation centres can be found throughout the country. They are, however, particularly prevalent within the inner cities where rates of conflict may be greater because of high-density living and the general stresses of the urban environment outlined above. Brown and Marriot (1993) argue that more affluent regions are more likely to experience disputes about boundaries and ugly buildings, but that noise disputes and conflict involving children are common across regions.

1.15 Mediation services vary in size and structure. Some rely exclusively on volunteers whereas others employ full-time staff whose activities may be supported by volunteers. Liebmann (1997) identifies a number of different organisational models for community mediation centres:

- firstly, housing associations and local authorities may train existing staff to mediate between tenants;

- secondly, they can use freelance mediators, although these may not be drawn from the local community;

- finally, mediation services can operate independently from the local authority or housing association.

1.16 Mediation UK has argued that the last option is the preferred model as it guarantees community involvement through management committee representatives and volunteer mediators. Moreover, they suggest that it helps build communication skills in the community by training local people in mediation techniques. The service is also more likely to be seen as impartial. The difficulties with the preferred model are that such organisations are vulnerable to funding pressures.

1.17   Community mediation centres also vary in their approach to mediation. The term 'mediation' tends to denote an ideological rationality rather than a single or homogenous identity and reflects a pluralistic rather than a monolithic concept (Bush and Folger 1994). Writing from an American perspective, Meschievitz (1991) has argued that the factors which shape mediation are so numerous that it is more helpful to view the practice as a style of approach rather than a specific model. In a similar vein, Metzloff (1992) has argued that 'mediation is one of the most overused but misunderstood terms in the ADR lexicon' (p.440). Definitions of mediation vary considerably and may conflict depending on mediators' ideologies, styles and practices; the scheme being considered; and whether the mediation provider is community or agency based; as well as, on the characteristics of the dispute (see, Bush 1989; Adler, Lovaas and Milner 1988; Levin and Golash 1985).[2] Bush and Folger have argued:

> *... the literature of the field reveals several very different accounts of 'stories' of the movement, told by different authors and stressing different dimensions of the mediation process and its societal impacts. Thus the movement is portrayed by some as a tool to reduce court congestion and provide 'higher quality' justice in individual cases, by others as a vehicle for organizing people and communities to obtain fairer treatment, and by still others as a covert means of social control and oppression. And some, including ourselves, picture the movement as a way to foster a qualitative transformation of human interaction. (p.17)*

They draw attention to three distinct 'stories' of the mediation movement told by proponents of the process.

- The satisfaction story – Mediation facilitates collaborative, integrative problem solving rather than adversarial distributive bargaining and can produce 'win-win' outcomes that reach beyond formal rights. As a result, it produces higher quality solutions than are possible in the courts.

- The social justice story – Mediation offers an effective means of organising individuals around common interests and thereby building stronger community ties. Because of its capacity for reframing issues and focusing on common interests, mediation can help individuals, who think they are adversaries, perceive a larger context in which they face a common enemy. In this way, it strengthens the weak by helping to establish alliances among them.

- The transformation story – Mediation has the capacity to transform the character of individuals and society. Its informality allows the parties to define problems and goals in their own terms. Mediation engenders acknowledgement and concern for 'adversaries'. Disputants are transformed from fearful defensive and self-centred beings into confident empathetic and considerate beings.

The literature on community mediation in the UK reveals traces of all these stories. However, it is significant that, although Bush and Folger claim that the transformation story is less frequently told, some figures in the 'movement' have identified an increasing tendency for community mediation centres to orientate their work towards this model.

Shared ideas

1.18 Despite the diversity of approaches to community mediation, a number of vague social and political ideals underlie the community mediation movement. These are the most frequently discussed parts of the stories highlighted above. Firstly, emphasis has been placed on the empowerment of local residents and the desirability of having individuals voluntarily resolve their own disputes. Empowerment is achieved by allowing the parties to take control of the resolution process. Private ordering is given moral superiority and the parties do not have to face the ritual of formal adjudication. Instead, they commonly find a community mediator who is dressed like them, sits with them round a table, talks like them or at least uses accessible language, and stresses help rather than threats. Such claims for empowerment have proven to be attractive to neo-liberal and neo-conservative critics of the welfare state who have expressed concerns about the culture of dependency it has created.

1.19 During the course of community mediation disputants are encouraged to provide a personal narrative detailing what it is that they want to achieve and to identify resolution options which are workable, achievable and acceptable by them. In this way, it is argued that mediation provides an opportunity for disputants to reject the intervention of the state and reclaim control over conflict resolution by choosing a settlement process which requires, rather than thwarts, their participation. Mediation allows people to resolve disputes according to frameworks which make sense to them rather than by reference to frameworks imposed by the state. Fuller (1971) has argued that mediation is commonly directed towards the creation of relevant norms rather than conformity to those supported by the formal legal system.

1.20 Secondly, emphasis is placed by proponents of community mediation on the importance of restoring peace and equilibrium to relationships. It has been suggested that, instead of polarising disputing parties into two enemy camps, mediation encourages them to focus on the problem between them. Community mediators stress the importance of focusing on common ground between the parties, looking to the future and accentuating the positive aspects of the disputants' relationship. The views of one mediator who took part in the research reported here reflect this approach:

> *What concerns me is when people are offered an amicable way to resolve a conflict and they choose not to take that option ... I embrace the fact that I am spreading peace. Not only am I doing a worthwhile job, but learning a great deal as I continue to be part of the SMC service. (SMC 1998)*

1.21   A third ideal is that of a grass-roots approach to disputes and an opposition to formal law. This reflects a distrust of governmental agencies as tending to impose bureaucratic, short-term or 'outside' solutions on the community. It has been argued that disputes managed by state officials are often allowed to run on with no consistent policy being followed. Rather than facilitating resolution, this can cause an escalation of the issues and an entrenchment of positions (Tebay *et al.* 1986).[3] This distrust of government agencies also extends to the courts which are viewed as unresponsive to the needs and interests of disadvantaged groups. Legal rules are seen as inflexible and unpragmatic as opposed to mediation which is responsive and flexible. Lawyers are viewed as elitist, expensive and responsible for the intensification of disputes because they treat them through the adversarial forms prescribed by the legal order and remove them from their natural context (Miller and Sarat 1980-1).

1.22   By encouraging such ideologies, proponents of mediation argue that the process helps individuals to become involved citizens within functioning communities. In this way it can be seen to underpin the requirements of a democratic society that people operate as free individuals. Thus, community mediation is implicated in a quest to revitalise communities by nurturing individual freedom. In the words of Brown and Marriot (1993):

> *Mediation schemes have been developing in Britain with the aim of bringing disputes arising within local communities under community control, thus avoiding the use of the legal system to deal with inter-personal or social agreements ... Far from being a second class service, such volunteers can bring knowledge of the local community, its cultures facilities and problems, and evidence of living there, to their mediation and for most neighbourhood conflicts this is a very valuable asset. It enables them to speak 'on the same wavelength' as the disputants and understand the unspoken undertones of their arguments. It makes them more acceptable to clients as being 'one of us'. (p.75)*

1.23   Shonholtz (1984) has argued that the suppression of conflict is destructive to the safety and vitality of communities and these ideals are reflected in the aims of the mediation centre being researched. As the co-ordinator wrote in the Centre's 1996/7 annual report:

> *One of our primary objectives when the Southwark Mediation Centre started was to create a situation where the service would become an integral part of community life. It has become clearly evident that the Centre if now fully established within Southwark. The reports from the project workers ... illustrate how broad and deep this work has gone. (SMC 1997 p.2)*

1.24 Working towards such goals is perhaps most evident in SMC's schools project which also stresses the preventative and educative functions of mediation as well as the 'organic integration' of the project within schools (SMC 1997, p.3).[4] As the schools project worker has argued:

> *Increasingly, it has been realised that for the mediation scheme to flourish, the whole school community needs to learn basic skills of conflict resolution and problem solving and to improve general social integration between pupil and pupil and ultimately between pupils and adults. (SMC 1997 p.3)*

1.25 These philosophies of empowerment, peace and individualism underpin practice across a variety of mediation models. The next section reviews the ways in which these abstract standards are translated into everyday practice.

The core features of practice

1.26 A number of core procedural features of mediation have been identified by proponents of the process (Murray, Rau and Sherman 1989; Roberts 1986; Black and Baumgartner 1983). These are that:

- mediation requires intervention by a neutral third party who facilitates bilateral negotiations between the principal parties to the dispute. This facilitation is said to be enhanced by the skills the mediator brings to the negotiation process. This approach can be compared to that of a judge who *imposes* a decision upon the parties;

- the mediator's authority derives from the parties. Mediators have no power to impose a decision on them. The parties are said to have a more substantial role than they would in court, including an opportunity to present their own argument. It follows from this that resolution is consensual, the only outcome being that which all parties agree upon;

- mediation aims to maximise the parties' interests. This may be done by taking into account remedies and concerns not recognised by the courts. The parties are *not bound by formal inflexible rules* such as those used by the courts. They may, for instance, make reference to common-sense notions of fairness;

- mediators adopt a problem-solving rather than an adversarial and confrontational approach to conflict, even though mediation often occurs in the shadow of the law and with reference to arguments constructed for use in an adversarial setting;

- any agreement should be *voluntarily* arrived at by the parties and it should be one with which they both feel satisfied. The belief is that the more satisfied the parties the more likely they are to abide by any agreement reached.

- finally, unless the parties decide to the contrary, mediation is a private and confidential process.

1.27   In subsequent chapters we will return to the issue of the extent to which this model can be achieved. In the remainder of this chapter the aims and methods of the research are outlined and the organisation of the report reviewed.

The aims and methods of the research

1.28   The main aim of the research reported here was to test the case for the use of mediation in the resolution of neighbour disputes. The effectiveness of mediation was adjudged by reference to the claims of mediators deriving from the three stories of mediation outlined above and the academic critiques of the practice discussed in the next chapter. The research was designed in such a way that it addressed a range of issues about the value of mediation raised by practitioners, policy makers and the academic community.

1.29   A number of different research methods were adopted in the research and these are summarised in tables 1.1 and 1.2 below. It can be seen from this that a mixture of qualitative (interviews and participant observation) and quantitative (analysis of case files, statistical analysis) methods have been used in the hope that this would give breadth and depth to the evaluation. All the key actors in managing housing disputes were involved in the research, including disputants, mediators and housing officers.

The organisation of this report

1.30   This report is split into ten chapters. The first four chapters provide background information to the project and set the scene for the data chapters which follow. Chapter 2 provides a critique of informal justice and community mediation.

It draws considerably on academic debates that have posed a number of questions which have proved important in the design and implementation of the evaluation. Chapter 3 provides some background information about Southwark Mediation Centre which contextualises many of the issues raised in subsequent chapters. The London Borough of Southwark is the site of much social deprivation and it is argued that neither the disputes which are mediated nor the approach of those mediating can be fully appreciated without an understanding of the environmental context. The period over which they have been the subject of research is one in which there has been much change in the organisational structure and policies of the Centre. The chapter attempts to chart these changes.

1.31 The next cluster of chapters presents the data collected for the project and a discussion of it. This section begins with chapter 4 and a review of the traditional management of disputes. It focuses on housing officers' views of their role and the ways in which they deal with disputes which are not referred to mediation. The final part of the chapter presents their views of the mediation process and their criteria for referral. Chapter 5 moves on to a discussion of the characteristics of disputes referred to mediation and goes on to discuss the ways in which many disputes are caused by factors external to the disputants. Chapter 6 reviews the workload of the mediation centre and the type and levels of mediator activity involved in their caseload. Chapter 7 considers processes used to resolve disputes through shuttle and face-to-face mediation. It also examines the mediation techniques used by SMC to achieve settlement of disputes. Chapter 8 looks at the various roles adopted by mediators and the challenge posed to them by the ideal that mediators should be neutral. Chapter 9 outlines the costs of mediation. The final chapter of the report concludes with a discussion of the major issues raised by the evaluation and poses questions for future research.

Endnotes

1. The state's responsibility to provide redress of citizen grievances is an obligation enshrined in the Magna Carta.

2. Mediation is used in several areas of the law, including family (see Davis 1988; Davis and Roberts 1988), commercial, neighbourhood (see, Dignan, Sorsby and Hibbert 1996) and international disputes.

3. Tebay *et al.*'s (1986) research shows that most complaints about neighbours are handled by housing assistants who did not always find their working methods to be effective.

4. SMC have reported instances of schools changing dramatically as a result of 'affective learning agendas' which include mediation being integrated into the life of the school. The improvements they have cited include enhanced academic achievements on the part of the pupils.

Table 1.1 Summary of methods

Original aim	Task completed	Problems experienced
Content analysis of case files kept by mediators (approx 200)	Content analysis of 207 paper case files completed (12 month's worth of cases) and 238 computerised files (a further 12 month's worth of cases)	Inconsistency in reporting of data. In particular, mediator activity was under-reported.
Case studies – analysis/observation of cases from referral to closure by SMC	Participant observations of 38 shuttle mediation visits.	This was a slightly lower number of case studies than originally anticipated but the data collected were more in-depth. A number of problems arose in achieving the original goal: (i) a high proportion of visits were cancelled by the disputants (20); (ii) changes within SMC increased mediator workloads and made inclusion of researchers a low priority. This made it difficult to follow complete cases.
Follow-up telephone interviews with disputants	17 interviews conducted with disputants	Problems with case studies (see above) meant that fewer disputants were identified. An alternative sample was identified but response rate remained low at 20%.
Interviews with housing officers across the entire borough	Interviews with 18 housing officers, including at least one officer from 14 (88%) of the 16 borough housing offices	There was a high turnover of housing officers although many of those we tried to contact had moved to another office within the borough.
Mediator interviews	Formal interviews throughout the project with the 4 mediators involved in housing disputes. Weekly Informal interviews conducted.	The mediators were extremely supportive of the project throughout.
Literature review	Interrogation of computerised databases, internet and traditional library sources	Potentially the literature on disputes and 'alternative methods' for resolution is massive. Very little empirical research undertaken. Most literature is from the United States.
Cost analysis	Interrogation of 247 electronic files held at SMC for housing and ES (12 month's worth)	These data became available towards the end of the project when SMC started to use electronic databases to record their activity on 'live' cases.

* The new sample was selected according to whether all three of the following criteria were met: 1. That the case was closed; 2. Mediation had not been rejected; 3. The person had been visited at least once.

† In one of the other housing offices, the mediation liaison officer had gone on maternity leave and a replacement had not been appointed. In the other offices, no mediation liaison officer had been appointed.

How was the problem resolved

Data were supplemented by more detailed records being kept at the request of the researchers. A form was designed for the purpose by the research team. One mediator provided sufficient information to estimate a real level of activity on 48 cases. Use was also made of a new database set up by SMC during the course of the study. This provided data on the time spent on 238 cases (12 month's-worth of cases).

Greater emphasis placed on participant observation of discrete visits to disputants. Transcripts generated and content analysis undertaken. This formed a much more important part of data collection than was originally anticipated and provided more detailed data than were specified in the original research proposal.

A different sample of disputants was identified from content analysis of paper files - 110 (1 year's-worth of clients) contacted*.

No alternative necessary. The data from interviews proved extremely valuable.

No alternative necessary.

No alternative necessary.

These data were supplemented with accounts from SMC annual reports and estimates made by mediators regarding the time spent on various duties they perform.

Table 1.2 Summary of additional methods

Additional methods adopted

Day-to-day shadowing of mediator activity	Participant observation of SMC mediators became an integral part of the project. On average, the research manager spent 3 days a week at SMC.	This allowed the research team to be privy to information which might not otherwise become available as a significant amount of trust built up between the research manager and SMC staff, This made the research manager conscious of the difficulty of maintaining objectivity.
Participant observation of face-to-face mediations	5 face-to-face mediations observed	It became apparent during the course of the research that face-to-face mediations did not occur as frequently as is suggested in the literature on community mediation. They hardly occurred at all during the period of reorganisation at the Centre. Not all the parties consented to have a researcher present.
Networking and *ad hoc* interviews	9 ad hoc interviews were undertaken with specialists in mediation and housing policy. During the course of the project, 2 conference papers were delivered on the subject.	

Research supervisor maintained more of a distance and only had connections with SMC staff during formal interviews,

Much more emphasis was placed on participant observation of visits.

Chapter 2: A critique of informalism and community mediation

The Chinese characters that make up the word 'conflict' are 'danger' and 'opportunity'. This demonstrates neatly the understanding that conflict is not necessarily destructive but is a vital part of change and growth, both of which can be painful.' (SMC 1998 p.10)

Introduction

2.1   In the last chapter we outlined the claims made by proponents of mediation about its possibilities. This chapter focuses on criticisms and concerns about mediation which have helped to frame the questions posed by the research. There is a reasonably clear divide between those who advocate and those who oppose the development of community mediation leading to what Pavlich (1996) has called 'a sterile impasse that encourages political apathy' (p4). Proponents of mediation often appeal to a Utopian vision of society and human relations. Whilst the aims of community mediation and its governing ideologies are laudable, there has been some concern about the ability of mediation to achieve such goals and provide a true alternative to the litigation system.

2.2   Given the extensive range of literature on mediation it is still relatively rare to find critics' evaluations of the process and it has been argued that negative evaluations have been left to a small number of left-wing academics (Delgado *et al*. 1985). This group have focused their concerns on four key issues:

●   the inability of community mediation to reach out to whole communities and heal community rifts;

●   a lack of success in reducing state control and empowering individuals;

●   a tendency to reinforce existing inequalities between disputants; and

●   over-emphasis on the value of peace.

2.3   In the remainder of this chapter each of these issues is considered in turn.

Healing community rifts?

2.4 A major concern of academic commentators has been the over-inflated claims that mediation can serve to heal community rifts, reduce community and individual alienation and prevent violent situations from escalating and build new alliances (see, for instance, Shonholtz 1984). These aspirations draw on the ideas of communitarian social thinkers and humanism which, in turn, rest on the belief that the social order depends on the voluntary acts of individuals who can choose to co-operate. In these visions of community, the cause of conflict lies within community and can be solved by members of the community. Socio-legal scholars have argued that the discussion of community in such contexts is a nostalgic one. An imaginary past community characterised by densely knit social relations and value consensus compared with modern disorder and community breakdown (see Abel 1982; Yngvesson 1996).

2.5 Critics have suggested that the ideological roles played by notions of 'community' are overused and under-defined. Ironically, given the context of the present research, it has been claimed that the ideal of community began to be utilised at exactly the time when the working class was fragmenting and communities ceased to be so consensual and harmonious (Matthews 1988). Evaluation of the pioneering work of the San Francisco Community Boards has suggested that mediation programmes have fostered the personal growth of mediator volunteers and engendered a sense of a transocial community of mediators linked by a common culture and maintained by shared practice. By way of contrast, surveys of local residents found no evidence of an increased or decreased sense of attachment to the neighbourhood as a result of the mediation programme (Yngvesson 1996).

2.6 Modern societies have high levels of mobility and cultural diversity and even where mobility is restricted it cannot be assumed that physical proximity alone creates cohesive communities. Communities may exist within geographical locations, but there may, in addition, be communities of understanding founded on such notions as gender, ethnicity, class, occupation, lifestyle, age and political beliefs. An emphasis on overarching notions of community may serve to blur intra-community disputes based on such things as ethnicity and class, issues which may only be understood within a historical context rather than as temporary skirmishes (see, for instance, Rothschild 1996). In addition, 'communitites' may be highly transient and this is especially the case in inner-cities. The norm within inner-cities is more likely to be heterogeneity than homogeneity. This may make the challenge of healing communities too great for mediators to tackle on their own (Merry 1990), if not impossible.

2.7 Concerns have been expressed that they have invited exposure to community issues and disputes. The disputes which are referred to mediation agencies may well be atypical of the types of conflict which arise in their community or communities. In their survey of 1062 householders, Karn *et al.* (1993) found that only two per cent of people with complaints about a neighbour would even threaten to report their neighbour to the local authority or police (see, also, General Accident 1995). More recently, Genn's (1999) large scale study of people with legal problems found that a minuscule proportion of those experiencing problems with their neighbours or landlord reported the matter to the council or other agency. This could mean that trying to understand community problems through data provided by formal or mediated disputes can present a skewed picture of the importance of formal voicing of grievances and the problems experienced within communities. Thus, an approach to dissatisfaction which uses disputes and complaints as a prism through which to understand community rifts may miss the usual in its search for publicly aired disputes. It is also clear that, even when disputes do become public, community mediation centres are just one of a number of agencies to which the dispute may be referred. Neighbour disagreements may also involve the police, the local housing office, environmental health and noise teams, legal and social services departments, citizen's advice bureaux, racial equality councils, local doctors, solicitors and the courts.

2.8 Pavlich (1996) has argued that the concept of community is unstable but that the notion is used by community mediators to carve out a general space or 'congregation' within which it seeks to regulate behaviour. 'Community' becomes a rhetorical device to encourage the use of symbols of shared identity, informalism, solidarity, freedom, harmony and hospitality, a place or buffer between the state and the individual (Pavlich 1996). But such visions may also serve to legitimate mediators' emphasis on the importance of harmony whilst simultaneously misrepresenting the ways in which people function within groups (Abel 1982; Yngvesson 1996).

Reducing state control?

2.9 Concerns have also been expressed about claims that mediation removes the state from the arbitration of disputes by giving control to the parties[1] and acts as an alternative to other processes such as the courts. Matthews has summed up the position of critics, thus:

> *The proliferation of local agencies penetrating deep into the heart of society and personal life, ultimately responsible to an ever unaccountable state bureaucracy, fuelled popular fears and anxieties about the totally administered society and the advent of 1984. Behind the engaging rhetoric of informalism the critics saw sinister motives. (Matthews 1988 p.9)*

2.10 Early critics of community mediation were deeply suspicious of the community mediation movement for the reason that it was commonly sanctioned by the very systems to which it sought to provide an alternative (Fitzpatrick 1992). Critics have claimed that the relationship between the formal and informal arena is not necessarily a complementary one, that is one sector contracting while the other expands. For Fitzpatrick (1992), informal processes reproduce some of the formality expected of the courts, provide a similar array of standards to be adhered to and reproduce power relations in ways which would be familiar to students of the litigation system. Abel (1982) has argued that rather than providing an alternative method of resolving disputes critics claim that there are a number of ways in which mediation can actually expand state control over the lives of ordinary people by introducing formalised state-sanctioned procedures for the handling of disputes which might previously have been ignored by state officials.

2.11 Conversely, for some, mediation facilitates the encroachment of state power into the private sphere of family and community life. For critics such as Fitzpatrick (1992), popular justice is but an extension of formal regulation, a 'mere mask or agent' (p. 199). Being a parallel service rather than an alternative one is particularly likely where core funding for mediation agencies comes from the state, as this brings with it a responsibility to process cases already lodged with state bodies and to account to them for the expenditure of funds and success of the scheme. Harrington's study of a neighbourhood justice centre demonstrated the ways in which informal processes have become supplemental agencies of the state. She showed that 88 per cent of cases referred to the neighbourhood centres she was researching came from prosecutors, judges or police who would otherwise have had to process the dispute and argued that, in this way, formal state resolution institutions retain some control over these disputes whilst offloading trivial conflicts to other agencies (Harrington, 1985).

2.12 A more serious concern of critics is that such expansion is made worse by the fact that many state agencies would otherwise be predisposed towards ignoring such trivial cases. Viewed in this way, informalism increases the exposure of disputants to state interference in their disputes and expands state control by bringing more cases into the dispute resolution arena. In his review of the American literature, Abel reminds us that, unlike formal institutions, informal ones rarely reject a case (Abel 1982). Moreover, in his recent review of neighbourhood mediation services Dignan suggested various ways in which community mediation 'claws in' new cases and expends money on cases which would otherwise not be the subject of protracted negotiations (Dignan *et al.* 1996).

Reinforcing existing inequalities?

2.13 It has also been argued that informalism encourages the further suppression of the disadvantaged and reinforces existing inequalities between disputants. This is significant since proponents of mediation have used the rhetoric of egalitarianism to justify their more conciliatory approaches to disputes and have argued that mediation promotes access to resolution services because of its informality. It is clear that mediation schemes have frequently been targeted at the disadvantaged and those who may already be getting a poor service from the court systems - people with violent partners; divorcing women; lay members of society challenging experts; and disputants who have not previously invoked the law. In a similar vein, Trubek has suggested that the growing interest in dealing with issues such as domestic violence out of the the courts can be seen as a reaction against the successes of the women's movement in their use of courts (Trubek 1980-1). In the US and UK, neighbourhood justice centres tend to be positioned in neighbourhoods with a disproportionate number of disadvantaged groups (Abel 1982). Research in a UK setting has indeed shown that disputes between neighbours are more likely to come from disadvantaged groups such as council tenants, women about men and from older people about younger people (Tebay *et al.* 1986). The needs of such groups may be ill-served by informal systems which emphasise the unravelling of feelings and meanings with a view to conciliation. Individualisation of grievances in these ways can undermine appreciation of a political or meta-narrative which may better serve to explain the causes of conflict within disadvantaged communities.

2.14 These concerns are exacerbated by the fact that many forms of informal resolution, community mediation included, discourage legal representation. In their extensive review of the literature on informalism and racial prejudice, Delgado *et al.* (1985) raise concerns that informalism increases the risk of unfair discrimination. Drawing on psychoanalytic theory and the socio-economic and political causes of prejudice, they argue that many people suffer from a moral dilemma which arises from a conflict between socially espoused precepts of equality and humanitarianism, and personal attributes and dispositions. The manner in which these conflicts are resolved depends largely on situational factors. They claim that certain settings such as mediation of intra-neighbour disputes serve to foster prejudiced behaviour because there are fewer formal powers available to check inappropriate conduct. Such disputes touch on sensitive or intimate areas of life which may be outside the ambit of formal rules and so increase the risk of outcomes being coloured by prejudice. By way of contrast they contend that the rules and structures of formal justice available in the courts serve to suppress bias.

2.15 Others have claimed that the appealing rhetoric of voluntarism, popular justice and individual empowerment disguises coercion within the mediation process. Hofrichter saw neighbourhood dispute resolution as being prompted by the need for changing projects to suppress working class resistance by encouraging conciliation within communities (Hofrichter 1982). Moreover, Silbey and Merry's (1986) study of a court-based and community-based mediation programmes suggests that mediators manipulate outcomes in subtle and covert ways by reinterpreting disputants' statements into euphemistic, morally neutral terms, selecting issues for discussion, 'concretising' some issues and postponing others which may raise more fundamental concerns about power imbalances or injustices. Grillo's (1991) work conducted in a family mediation context also stresses the ways in which women are disadvantaged in informal settings because they often serve to impose a subtle but rigid orthodoxy as to how they should behave.

2.16 In a UK context, important work by Greatbatch and Dingwall (1989) on divorce mediators suggests that the process of mediation can be used to press weaker parties into accepting less than they could have expected had their case gone through overtly adversarial channels. They argue that, despite claims to the contrary, disputants can be guided towards outcomes that the mediators rather than the parties find most appropriate. Mediators in their empirical study were labelled 'selective' facilitators. They regularly exerted pressure in favour of certain options over others, encouraged discussion in certain directions and inhibited exploration of other issues (Greatbatch and Dingwall 1989). Critics have maintained that such covert coercion is detrimental to the parties' interests because properly recognised coercion stimulates resistance and justifies the demand for the protection of formal due process. Viewed in this way mediation is more pernicious because its sources are less obvious and points of resistance less clearly defined.

The value of peace?

2.17 Critics of mediation have expressed concern that community mediation may place too much emphasis on getting opposing parties to acknowledge 'shared' values and resolve their dispute on the basis of them. Peace emerges from the literature as something of a moral imperative in the mediation process. It is contended by proponents that informal systems can operate to defuse the anger of disputants. Anger is seen as destructive and mediation purports to offer solutions in which no one wins and no one loses. Thus, there is a predisposition to compromise and conflict is depicted as a failure of communication or a misunderstanding. Emphasis is put on the cathartic effect of mediation; and on expressive rather than instrumental functions.

2.18 Colson has argued that the claim that disputes should be resolved and that resolution leads to harmony is a Western construct derived from Christianity. She contends that this arouses expectations that reconciliation and the restoration of social harmony are considered to be the ideal condition for human beings. These criticisms have not only been levelled at practitioners (Colson 1995). Cain and Kulcsar (1982) criticise academics for their assumptions of ideological functionalism or the reformist desire to eliminate disputes.

2.19 Critics of the orientation towards peace are concerned that mediation serves to underplay the conflicts between powerful and less powerful groups in society such as social landlords and impoverished tenants. Fundamental disagreement about social and political values cannot feature as a dominant issue when emphasis is placed on the individualisation of the dispute, discrete events and communication failures. In this way, informalism can have the effect of siphoning discontent from the courts and in reducing the risk of political confrontation which might bring about valuable social change (Fiss 1984). The result is the preservation of the stability of the social system. In these ways informalism can be seen to serve private interests at the expense of public ones and unlike adjudication fail to make public the debate about conflicting ideologies.

2.20   Nader (1980) has put the case that it is unlikely that the force of law can be marshalled to address 'little injustices' unless they are reconceptualised as collective harms. Adler *et al.* (1988) argue that emphasis is placed on wholeness rather than fragmentation:

> *There is nothing about rights and claims, about neighbourhoods fighting city hall in the name of justice, or about the ethnic lawyer rising out of (but still practising in) the old neighbourhood to fight the big boys downtown, or for that matter, to join the big boys downtown and become a member of the successful political machine. (p.123)*

The very construction of a dispute as a 'neighbourhood' dispute could be seen to lay emphasis on the intra-community aspects of the dispute rather than issues of importance between the state and its citizenry. The state emerges as the dispute processor rather than as one of the parties.

Conclusion

2.21   The criticisms of mediation reviewed in this chapter pose a serious and important challenge to proponents of mediation and have provided a template of issues against which to interpret the data collected for the study reported here. Critics have argued convincingly that, despite the goals of mediation, its growth may have the effect of increasing state intervention in people's lives and exacerbate the inequalities that exist between disputants. It has also been argued that an over-emphasis on peaceful and conciliatory settlement of disputes in a private setting reduces the potential for disputes to challenge the way things are. This is a particularly pertinent concern for the disadvantaged residents of Southwark who may be amongst the most likely members of the population to want to see changes in their relationship with their landlord and the material conditions in which they live. In particular, research into community mediation has suggested that the state is often implicated in the cause of disputes. By conceptualising complaints about such problems as disputes between neighbours the state avoids direct challenges about such issues as the quality of its social housing.

2.22 But, for some, critics of mediation have presented too pessimistic a view of its potential to resolve disputes and create an equilibrium within communities. It is noticeable that despite their concerns critics of informalism rarely deny the possibility of popular justice or the potential of mediation. The same writers have also been highly critical of the ability of the courts to deal with community disputes sensitively and effectively. Have critics of mediation been overly zealous in their assertions about encroaching state control? Have they remained insensitive to the possibility of community mediation facilitating change within communities? These issues will be revisited throughout the report. It will be argued that a way to theorise about mediation can be found which recognises its constraining potential alongside its ability to instigate change.

Endnote

1.   Of this group, Richard Abel's various publications on the issue provide some of the most important and influential treatments of the subject. He has identified a number of issues which should remain at the forefront of evaluations by law and society scholars (see, in particular, Abel, 1982).

Chapter 3: About Southwark Mediation Centre

Introduction

3.1 This chapter provides a profile of Southwark Mediation Centre (SMC) and explains why it has a high profile within the mediation community. The chapter is in three parts. The first section reviews the various projects with which SMC has become involved. The second section considers the various ways in which increased levels of funding and structural re-organisation have facilitated a new focus for the mediators. In the final section, the implications of change for the future are considered.

Location and staffing

3.2 Southwark is a borough which is marked by diversity. One of the most deprived in London, yet it has pockets of affluence; a rich mix of cultures; and hosts stable communities alongside transient populations. The London Borough of Southwark is situated at the heart of London. It suffered extensive bomb damage during the war of 1939-45 with the result that after the war there was a huge amount of high-rise development. The majority of housing comes in the form of purpose-built flats (63 per cent) and this is complemented by terraced houses (19 per cent); converted or partly converted accommodation (13 per cent); semi-detached houses (four per cent); and detached houses (one per cent). Southwark has a higher percentage of purpose-built flats (82 per cent) than any other inner-city borough except for Tower Hamlets (OPCS 1991).

3.3 Resident in the borough of Southwark suffer from worse living conditions than are the norm in Greater London and England as a whole. In the later years of the last century, industry has substantially deserted the area, a development seen most dramatically in the closure of the docks. Road improvements, such as at the Elephant and Castle, have contributed to a bleak urban landscape in some areas of the borough. A significant number of residents are unemployed and it has a high proportion of teenage single parents (eight per cent of households). The proportion of unemployed and economically inactive people in the borough is high and rates are above the average for all London inner-city boroughs. Poor living conditions in the borough have attracted sizeable grants for large-scale housing initiatives from charitable trusts, the government and the European Community.

3.4   As London's largest council landlord, Southwark manages 54,477 homes and a very large proportion of residents in Southwark rent their accommodation from the local authority (51 per cent). This compares with an average of 34 per cent of residents in inner-city London and 23 per cent for Greater London. The rate of owner occupation in Southwark is much lower than in London as a whole and less than half the national average. Eighty-two per cent of homes (44,421) are in purpose-built blocks of flats higher than three stories (Southwark Council 1996). This compares with 15 per cent in the UK as a whole (Office for National Statistics 1999).

3.5   In recent years Southwark has been experiencing a rapid and unprecedented process of change and debate about how regeneration is best achieved continues. Southwark Council's Regeneration Statement (Southwark Council 1999) encompasses housing, education, employment and the environment and points the way forward to achieving the highest standards in these areas. As a result, large sections of the borough have undergone considerable restructuring and there has been a significant shift from high to low density housing. Many of the unpopular high density estates of the 1960s and 1970s are being refurbished or demolished and replaced with new streets and houses

3.6   SMC is a registered charity based on a major road to the north of the London Borough of Southwark in a large period house. The centre was established in 1985 with funding from the Greater London Council (GLC). In 1986 funding transferred from the GLC to Southwark Council when the regional council for London was abolished. The Centre is well known within the mediation community. A number of characteristics mark it out as special. It was one of the first centres of its kind to open and is now one of the largest in terms of the throughput of cases and staffing levels. Unlike many of its counterparts, SMC is increasingly relying on paid workers rather than volunteers. This has been made possible by a high reliance on external grants. SMC has received funding from a number of sources, including the Single Regeneration Budget, the Gulbenkian Foundation, Southwark Education and Leisure Department, Southwark Housing Department and Southwark Public Protection Service. In addition, it has become renowned for some of its pioneering work such as its school mediation schemes (Brown and Marriott 1993).

3.7   Staff at the Centre also characterised their work by reference to the distinctiveness of their approach. There was a recognition amongst staff at the Centre that SMC's approach to disputes differed from that of other mediation centres. SMC deals with a number of types of dispute that other community mediation centres have not or are not prepared to deal with. These include cases involving race, assaults, homophobic harassment and criminal damage (SMC 1997). In many ways this reflected a pragmatic approach to dispute resolution. Mediators were unwilling to refer cases to other agencies where this would, in their view, lead to ineffective resolution. One of the mediators also argued that a lack of trust between some members of the local community and the police means that many issues referred to them would not be pursued if the 'victim' felt that they would be encouraged to take the matter up with the police direct. Whilst the value of having such cases dealt with by agencies with coercive powers was recognised if aggressors were to be punished, it was also argued that the majority of 'victims' would not be prepared to pursue their case through more official channels such as the courts.

3.8 The centre has a full-time co-ordinator who undertakes some mediating, six full-time mediators, two part-time mediators and a full-time administrator. The staff are supported in their work by a team of eight fully-trained volunteers. Without exception, all the paid mediators at SMC were previously connected with the Centre as volunteer mediators and all the mediators continue to devote at least six hours a month to the centre as unpaid volunteers. In addition, staff receive the advice and assistance of a management committee made up of representatives from the local community.

The work of the Centre

3.9 Mediators at the Centre have experience in handling conflict in a number of different settings including:

- neighbour mediation;

- family mediation;

- business mediation;

- victim/offender schemes;

- schools mediation;

- restorative justice.

In addition to these funded initiatives, the agency is also involved in a number of other mediation-related activities such as training and dissemination of information about mediation.

3.10 Staff at the Centre now manage five major projects although we concentrate in this report on those involving neighbour disputes: Housing, Environmental Services and Five Estates projects. There is considerable overlap between these initiatives. The distinguishing feature between them is the method of referral and the funding body. The Five Estates Project focuses on the needs of five particularly impoverished estates in the borough and handles referrals from a variety of agencies about any type of neighbour dispute within the Five Estates boundary. By contrast, the Housing Project only receives referrals about neighbour disputes from Housing Offices, some of whom may operate within the Five Estates Area. The Environmental Services Project receives referrals about noise from the Environmental Services Department which operates across the borough. This means that a noise dispute in the Five Estates could be referred to SMC under any of the three projects. Outside the Five Estates area a noise dispute could only be referred under the Housing or Environmental Project.

The Housing project

3.11   This is the biggest project managed by the Centre and has been running since 1985, funded by the GLC and then Southwark Council. It has a dedicated co-ordinator and case worker. The project is funded to accept up to 150 referrals a year from 16 housing offices across the borough. Housing officers can refer any dispute between neighbours in the borough which has been presented to them for resolution. i.e. where one neighbour has formally complained about another. Each housing office has appointed a mediation liaison officer to facilitate communication with SMC.

Environmental Services project

3.12   SMC also receives funding from the Environmental Services department (ES), a centralised council department, to take up to 110 referrals every year from its officers. The department handles direct complaints from residents about environmental issues, such as noise pollution and rubbish. It operates a 24-hour emergency noise nuisance service which residents can call upon to request an immediate investigation. Domestic noise problems increasingly dominate the ES noise team's resources and account for about 80 per cent of all complaints received (Southwark Council 1999).

The Five Estates project

3.13   This is an initiative which is funded in part by the European Union Single Regeneration Budget. It focuses on the five estates within the borough which have been targeted as part of the £250million regeneration of Peckham. Referrals to the mediation agency can be accepted from a number of borough-wide parties including housing associations, the police, tenants' associations, tenant management committees and individual residents. Because this project focuses on a geographical area rather than a particular type of problem it has allowed SMC to promote mediation to particular groups, such as women's groups, tenants associations, ethnic minorities and senior citizens (SMC 1997). An offshoot of the project has been the development of a newsletter targeted at the police called

Bill Board. This attempts to generate interest in mediation amongst the police. It gives anonymised accounts of recent cases, results and explains how to refer cases to the agency.

Other projects

3.14   SMC has also been becoming increasingly involved in school's mediation as more and more people seek to introduce children and young people to the skills of conflict resolution and mediation. The Centre was one of the first agencies to move into this field, although a number of other mediation centres now provide similar services. The aim of this initiative has been to train pupils to mediate disputes between other pupils and so contribute to improving the social atmosphere of the school as well as the interpersonal skills of the students involved (SMC 1997). A number of schools have become involved in the initiative and received training from SMC mediators. A knock-on effect of this work has been an increased awareness among mediators of the need to involve children in the mediation of other disputes in which they are involved in a different context, e.g., inter-family neighbourhood disputes. In one recent case, cited in the SMC annual report, conflict between the parents of neighbouring families and between the children resulted in the parents going to mediation and the children (aged between 11 and 12) having a separate mediation in which they made their own agreement.

3.15   The Centre has also been successful in attracting funding for a restorative justice project from the Youth Offending Team of the Home Office. This new project was launched in October 1999 and involves the Centre in victim offender work and family conferencing. Referrals are Southwark-based although victims or offenders may have been relocated around the country.

Changes at the Centre – funding and visibility

3.16   In the last five years, Southwark Mediation Centre has undergone a number of changes. The variety of projects now being managed by the Centre has brought with it a significant increase in income and this has improved working conditions. In September 1996, the Centre faced a possible deficit at the end of the year. The Chair of the management committee reported that staff were underpaid, had no pension scheme and no proper job security (SMC 1997). Just three years later the Centre's accounts show a healthy balance. Moreover, the structures and policies of the Centre have been reviewed and salaries allocated on a much more egalitarian basis. The increase in their workload is such that staff are having to contemplate moving to larger premises.

3.17 The Centre has come to rely much more heavily on funding from the Council. Many community organisations remain sceptical about accepting state funding for fear of being too beholden to state agencies. Commentators on community mediation have argued that too much reliance on a small number of grants can have its costs in terms of independence and flexibility. But alternative funding can be hard to come by and, as a result of their concerns, many community mediation organisations remain little more than a loose amalgam of volunteers, processing a relatively small number of cases. Staff at SMC were aware of the potential dangers of accepting too much state funding but had also been enthused by the possibilities created by more stable financial support. In response to concerns about independence, they had adopted a policy of ensuring that their funding came from a variety of council departments and other government agencies.

3.18 Their strategy has considerable benefits. The upturn in income and number of paid staff has brought with it a form of financial and job security not experienced by workers at the Centre before. This means that they have been able to organise their activities in line with a more professional model than was ever possible before. One mediator described how the increase in stability meant that the experienced staff could be more supportive of new colleagues and offer proper 'apprenticeships' to staff. It has also been suggested that they are also much better placed to retain and headhunt staff. In addition, this stability has also meant that they could experiment with more flexible working hours and that, in turn, has allowed them to take on mediators with different types of responsibilities and life experiences from established mediators, such as parents with young children.

3.19 The issue of independence from funders was raised with all the mediators at the Centre in interviews and they were all convinced that they were not compromised by the source of their grants. Firstly, they argued that they still had a variety of sources of income. Secondly, their premises were not owned by the council. Finally, attention was also drawn to the fact that their reporting duties were not onerous and the council had no representatives on their management committee. Only one mediator claimed they had ever felt compromised by the nature of SMC's relationship to the council but this arose as a result of the duty of confidentiality to clients rather than as a result of funding.

3.20 The new stability has also had an impact on the confidence of those working within the organisation. The current co-ordinator described the rate of growth of SMC as 'quite frightening'. A colleague of hers agreed: 'It still feels quite strange. We used to have to go and knock on doors, now organisations come to us. We automatically got put into two recent SRB bids.' In a similar vein, another SMC mediator reflected:

Twelve years ago we were offering mediation to a population who had little knowledge of what mediation was, let alone its ability to help in their situation. If they said no, we had little to offer in response to prove that mediation works as experience of community mediation in the whole of the UK was very limited. Now, our successes are many and the pressure from referring agencies to deliver a result has increased. (SMC 1997 p.10)

3.21   The increased level of interest in their activities is not just manifesting itself in Southwark. The Centre has had inquiries from community workers and policy makers from Germany, Portugal, Ghana, Greece and Israel about their work. In addition, where they had once felt rather isolated, staff were now of the opinion that they were becoming increasingly well connected within community mediation networks and better able to participate in national and regional events.

Towards a professional service?

3.22   With these changes in the workload have come changes in approach. There was a recognition amongst staff that over the time they were being evaluated, they had moved towards a more regularised and sophisticated service. As their fund-raising activities have increased, they have been much more successful in attracting core funding. They have also become more conscious of information technology. All staff now have access to a computer and the centre now maintains a computerised database on the bulk of its cases. Mediators have also been able to devote more time to the training of volunteers.

3.23   The Centre now places much more emphasis on using paid mediators than was previously the case and the ratio of paid staff to unpaid volunteers is much higher than it was five years ago. Such policies are not without their critics as there is an argument that it is through the use of volunteers, who live and work within the communities being served, that mediation agencies maintain their links with them and remain grounded. However, Southwark mediators felt that the extensive use of volunteers also had its disadvantages and made the service less reliable. Five main reasons were cited for this.

●   It takes much longer for volunteers to acquire mediation skills and they are often unable to mediate on a regular basis. One of the paid mediators commented that she had learnt more in one year as a member of staff than she had in six years as a volunteer.

●   The receipt of council funding provided incentives to increase the use of paid staff. Not only is the income available to fund their posts, but paid mediators were unwilling to give cases to volunteers to manage when paid staff retained the responsibility to account for the progress of their caseload.

- There is a lot of work involved in co-ordinating volunteers and it can be difficult to make sure that they are involved in a case from start to finish.

- Housing officers tend to build up a relationship more easily with paid project workers because they are available in office hours and will specifically ask for them to mediate a dispute.

- Finally, SMC is using the technique of shuttle mediation more and more, in preference to the traditional form of mediation which occurs face to face. Shuttle mediation makes more demands on volunteers who may not always be available to undertake visits to both parties homes.

3.24 A new role for volunteers has been identified. The Centre has recently adopted a policy of co-mediation as a result of concerns about the safety of mediators working alone at night in rough parts of the borough. The policy change is resource-hungry requiring as it does a doubling-up of paid workers. However, at the time the research was being completed, staff were considering making increased use of volunteer staff to shadow paid mediators. This obviates the need for the same volunteer to attend at each stage of the mediation as continuity is provided by the paid mediator who attends.

3.25 During the course of the research project, SMC had also started to take on mediators from outside the borough. By the end of the project four of the paid mediators were living in the borough in council or ex-council properties and another four lived outside, although one had lived in the borough for a substantial proportion of their life. This new approach did not meet with universal approval within the Centre. Whilst proponents of this move felt that mediation skills and personality traits could be transferred across London boroughs and that the most important thing was that workers were 'street wise', others felt that many of Southwark's problems were unique and much better understood by those with established local roots.

Conclusion

3.26 In this chapter we have outlined the various activities of SMC and attempted to plot the various changes which have occurred to the Centre since we first started our research. The period over which we have been evaluating the Centre has been one in which there have been many policy changes and alterations to levels of funding. At times this has caused difficulties for the research team as we have had to adapt the research to analysis of different working methods as they have been introduced. But the gradual professionalisation of the Centre has also had its pay-offs. The computerisation of records has meant that there is data which has become available to analyse, the introduction of new staff has meant that there has been a richer discussion of issues. The development of mediator apprenticeships and training programmes has caused mediators to be more reflexive about what marks the centre out and what their approach to mediation amounts to. The impression is of an organisation which has grown in confidence.

3.27 The changes instigated at SMC have facilitated an experiment in alternative more professionalised provision of community mediation services. For this very reason, the changing emphasis will also attract criticisms from those committed to a more traditional model of provision. Particular targets for criticism are likely to be: the recruitment of mediators from other more affluent London boroughs; the changes in the use of volunteers (specifically encouraged by council funding) such as new conceptions of ownership of the case; and the creation of a hierarchy between paid mediators and volunteers suggested by the new co-mediation policy. For some, these changes will be interpreted as the state beginning to colonise this form of popular justice. The theme is one to which we return.

Chapter 4: Management of disputes by housing officers

4.1　In order to place this evaluation of community mediation in context, it is important to be able to compare mediation with more traditional models of dispute resolution. This facilitates a consideration of how the disputes referred to Southwark Mediation Centre (SMC) might otherwise have been handles and the relative merits and disadvantages of mediation as compared to these other methods. The focus of the chapter is on the work of housing officers. The vast majority of disputes handled by SMC are referred by housing officers after a formal complaint has been lodged by one tenant about another.

4.2　The chapter starts by considering the incidence of neighbour disputes in the borough and the interface between formal and informal processing of disputes. Secondly, it considers the formal resolution options available to council officials other than mediation. The third section considers the role of the housing officer and the model of dispute handling adopted by them. In section four, the circumstances in which housing officers consider referring cases to mediation are reviewed along with their views about the benefits of handling cases in that way. The final section presents the views of SMC mediators about the referrals they receive. The chapter makes it clear that housing officers occupy a pivotal role in determining how a case will be processed. They have a considerable discretion as to how a case should be managed and act as gatekeepers to SMC. The success or failure of the mediation scheme is largely dependent on their co-operation.

How many disputes reach the council?

4.3　Previous studies have suggested that social landlords keep very few records on the number, time and resolution of disputes between their residents (see Aldbourne Associates 1993; and Dignan *et al.* 1996). In our interviews with housing officers we found that records were kept on an ad hoc basis, with only four of the 14 housing offices indicating that they kept comprehensive records on disputes. It was suggested by some that reports were only kept in the more 'serious' nuisance cases, where the problem was considered a form of harassment (HO6). Attempts have been made by the council to instigate a more centralised database of statistics on cases referred and action taken. A financial incentive has even been offered to housing offices which use and return 'case plans' on dispute management for this purpose. However, at the time the present study was completed there had been little support for the project at housing officer level and borough wide data remains woefully inadequate.

4.4   The lack of data on the number of disputes referred to housing officers makes it difficult to compile a picture of the proportion of all cases which are referred to mediation. However, recent research conducted by Hazel Genn (1999) for the Nuffield Foundation does give some indication of the number of disputes which arise between neighbours which come to the attention of formal state agencies such as the council. In her random sample of 4125 adults she discovered that 40 per cent had experienced one or more 'justiciable' problem during the previous five years. Of the total population seven per cent had experienced problems living in rented accommodation. This translates as 124 problems per 1000 head of the population over 18. The main problems in this category were trying to get the landlord to undertake repairs, followed by disputes with neighbours. If these statistics are used to calculate the number of grievances which arise between neighbours in Southwark, it can be surmised that 24,428 such grievances arise every five years across the borough.

4.5   Interestingly, the research also revealed that respondents in the survey had taken some action to try and resolve the problem in about 89 per cent of cases. Two thirds (69 per cent) had written or spoken to the other side about the problem and over a third (37 per cent) had sought formal advice. Mediation or the services of an ombudsman had been used in none of these cases. However, it was shown that:

- 45 per cent of all those experiencing problems had contacted their local authority at one time or another;

- 27 per cent had contacted the police;

- 25 per cent had been in touch with solicitors and;

- 25 per cent had sought the advice of Citizen's Advice Bureau.

4.6 These data suggest that a fairly high proportion of disputes involving landlords or neighbours come to the attention of the council but that few go on to become formal disputes capable of being referred to mediation. It would seem that disputants are more likely than not to deal with a neighbour grievance without invoking the help of the council and that, even when the council is involved, the majority of cases do not escalate sufficiently to become classified as 'serious' disputes. These data reflect the findings of a number of other socio-legal research projects which have revealed that disputes which become classified as formal by state agencies are atypical (Miller and Sarat 1980-1; Mulcahy and Tritter 1998). The phenomena revealed by these data are represented in pictorial form in figure 4.1

Figure 4.1 Formal complaints are just the tip of a disputes iceberg

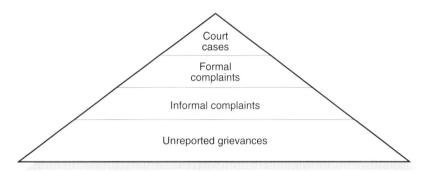

4.7 Data collected from Environmental Services (ES) in Southwark also go some way to developing a map of the incidence of disputes in the borough. ES receives in the region of 12,000 complaints about noise in a year (Murphy 2000).[1] Table 4.1 shows a breakdown of all the noise related complaints received by ES over a six-month period in 1999. It can be seen from this that the vast majority of complaints relate to domestic noise within households caused by stereo equipment.

Table 4.1 Noise complaints recorded by Southwark noise team from April-September 1999

Type of noise recorded by noise team	No. of incidences	Percent
Domestic music	4378	65
Domestic other e.g. DIY/banging/shouting	605	9
Premise's alarm sounding	319	5
Construction site noise	280	4
Entertainment noise	251	4
Church/community centres	157	2
Car alarm	138	2
Domestic animals – dogs, birds	128	2
Commercial noise	96	1
Bonfire	77	1
Event/fair/festival	61	1
Road construction noise	43	1
Dust from construction/demolition	35	0
Industrial noise	26	0
Odour/fume – commercial/industrial	11	0
Odour/fumes – residential	9	0
Noise in the street – not car alarm	5	0
Ice cream chimes – mobile	0	0
Other noise pollution	119	2
Total	**6738**	**99**

4.8 One mediator at SMC reported that only 40 per cent of these complaints are new with 60 per cent of disputes being between parties who have previously come to the attention of the service (M5). These data suggest that many disputes continue to fester after they have been brought to the attention of state agencies and few are resolved. Noise team representatives have also indicated that their impression is that the majority of complaints are by immediate neighbours (Murphy 2000).[2]

To what is mediation an alternative?

4.9   There are a number of ways of resolving neighbour disputes and a number of individuals and agencies that might become involved in their resolution (see figure 4.2). As far as formal powers are concerned, local authorities have wide powers to deal with neighbour nuisance and noise under the Environmental Protection Act 1990, the Noise and Statutory Nuisance Act 1996 and the Housing Act 1996. Under the Environmental Protection Act 1990 it became a duty of local authorities to take all reasonably practicable steps to investigate a complaint of statutory nuisance. Additionally, local authorities are obligated to serve an abatement notice on the perpetrator if they are satisfied there is evidence of noise nuisance. Tenants may also make their complaints to local housing officers who can invoke the tenancy agreement's clauses about quiet enjoyment to discourage anti-social behaviour. The 1996 Housing Act also introduced probationary, or introductory, tenancies giving local authorities increased power to seek possession whilst tenants are on these contracts. Under the same Act local authorities could start possession proceedings on existing tenants through a 'fast-track' system, making eviction more accessible (Dignan *et al.* 1996). Finally, under the Crime and Disorder Act non-residents/visitors who cause a nuisance have become the responsibility of the tenant, although social landlords may be reluctant to seek possession under these circumstances.

4.10   The police have a minimal role in neighbour and noise nuisance, landlord and tenant and other 'non-criminal' disputes. Chief Inspector Tony London from Southwark has reported that 'civil dispute, advice given, no cause for action' is the most likely police response to these problems. Police advice given most often refers the aggrieved party to a civil remedy - an application for a county court summons or private summons from the magistrates court (SMC 1998).

4.11   Officers from the Environmental Services noise nuisance team patrol streets in the borough investigating complaints about noisy neighbours. This is part of a 24-hour 'reactive service'. Once a person asks the council to investigate a complaint, two officers will go to the address in question to gauge the level of noise. Officers aim to visit within one hour in order to witness the alleged noise (Murphy, 2000). If they feel the noise level is unreasonable, they will ask the occupant to be quieter. This can be followed up by a simple cautionary letter or a legal notice requiring the occupant to keep noise levels to a minimum in future. Such measures are usually invoked where the person involved refuses to reduce their noise or repeats it.[3] In extreme cases, a notice can be served immediately and this can be followed up by immediate prosecution. Officers also have the power to confiscate musical equipment if they feel that is the only way to stop the noise. A prosecution will lead to a court appearance and a possible fine of £5,000 for individuals and £20,000 for commercial bodies. The noise team reported in 1995 that an average of 160 notices for night nuisance alone are served every year and, of these, 50 will go to court.

Figure 4.2 Routes of resolution

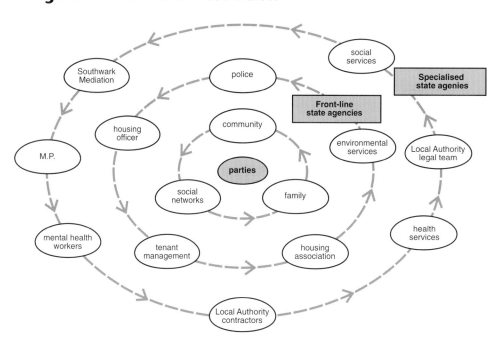

4.12 Legal action of this kind is much more likely to result in a favourable outcome for the council than legal action instigated by housing officers under the tenancy agreement. The presence of a professional witness from the noise nuisance team undoubtedly reduces the evidential burden of the council. As one noise nuisance officer indicated:

> *We are not reluctant to take legal proceedings and also undertake seizures of noise-making equipment. We invariably prosecute where we have seized equipment and request forfeiture of the equipment at the hearing. The court usually grants forfeiture orders and we can sell the equipment and use income to offset storage costs. (Murphy 2000 p.14)*

4.13 Where the noise team becomes involved in complaints about noise, mediation is much more likely to occur in the shadow of formal legal procedures, when a prosecution is less likely to succeed. Noise team officers are encouraged to refer cases to mediation only where one party is agreeable, where there is no legal remedy (such as defective sound insulation or children's noise) or where the team is unlikely to be able to obtain evidence because of the short duration of the noise.

The role of the housing officer

4.14   Since the vast majority of disputes referred to SMC came from the housing project, the remainder of this chapter focuses on these referrals. Interviews with housing officers were used to explore how they viewed their role in neighbour disputes, the sort of cases they considered it appropriate to refer to mediation and the way disputes were managed when they were not referred to SMC. The role of the housing officer and the officers' perception of their role varied from housing office to housing office but most were concerned that the job had become less personalised in recent years. Most interviewees made particular reference to the fact that their job had changed significantly since housing services had been 'contracted out'. In many cases, this had led to redundancies and a rationalisation of services. The housing officers interviewed felt that their workload was much heavier as a result. One implication of this cited by several interviewees was that they did not have as much time as they had previously to walk round the estates for which they were responsible. In turn, many mentioned that they did not get to know tenants as well as they had once been able to. Contracting out of their services has led to increased specialisation of officers. A number felt that this made the service more efficient but were concerned that it did not give them a sufficiently holistic perspective on the needs of tenants. Some housing officers suggested that the changes had de-personalised the service and altered the tenants' first 'port of call'. Many disputes are now handled by front-line customer care staff who staff the inquiry desks rather than by dedicated estate managers as was previously the case. Few of the housing officers were happy about the changes. As one officer explained:

> *We are their priest, their doctor, their counsellor, their friend. Many tenants see us as a god, there to provide them with all they need. They don't really understand about contracting out and how our role has changed. They just know that I am [Bert] and that I will help them get things sorted out. It may be unfashionable but these people have needs and I rather think that addressing them is what I should be doing.*

4.15   Housing officers admitted that in many cases referred to them they had very little chance of actually resolving the dispute. Recent research has confirmed that the incidence of unresolved landlord and tenant or neighbour disputes was high when compared with other types of justiciable issues. Genn's (1999) survey revealed that 70 per cent of such cases remained unresolved. One housing officer estimated that they resolved no more than 10 per cent of complaints.

Stages in the dispute-handling process

4.16 When asked about their management of disputes between neighbours, housing officers identified three main stages in handling complaints. These were: understanding the issues in dispute; the sending of a formal letter; and legal action. Their choice of options varied with the nature of the dispute and reflect the use of both formal and informal management methods.

1. Understanding the issues in dispute

4.17 For the majority of housing officer, the first stage in trying to sort out a complaint would be to attempt to resolve it themselves. Many of the housing officers indicated that their first job was to try and understand what was behind tenants' grievances. They saw themselves as providing a useful audience which could allow a complainant to explore their emotions and voice their concerns. In the words of one housing officer: 'I let them pour out what they want to.' Most officers talked through the allegations with the complainant and the person being complained about. The exception to this was where there was independent evidence from the council's noise team in which case most housing officers would send a formal letter out straight away (see below). But, in the majority of cases, the parties would be interviewed separately in the housing office about the allegations. Less often, the housing officer would visit the parties in their homes.

4.18 Many officers mentioned that they used these meetings to try and understand the context within which the dispute had arisen and to make suggestions about action which could be taken to improve things. One officer described how she would go and visit each property involved before coming to any conclusion as some disputes were precipitated by living conditions, such as poor plumbing. In these cases, a simple repair could solve the problem. In a number of other cases, officers felt that there were often a range of other issues below the surface which had prompted the conflict. It was the majority view that disputes were commonly more complex than they initially appeared. This tended to be because the dispute had a long and multi-faceted history. As one officer explained:

> *You use the softly, softly approach at first. You get the story from the complainant, but you must remember that they could be telling on someone else to divert the attention away from them[selves]. I tend to gather my information from various sources and people at this stage.*

4.19 In many areas, complainants are encouraged to keep a diary of disturbances. The housing officer may also refer the case to the noise team and request them to collect evidence of the disturbances being complained about. Such evidence can prove to be important if the housing officer decides to progress to a more formal way of dealing with the dispute.

2. Formal letter

4.20　If the dispute could not be resolved after an interview with both parties then resolution methods moved quite quickly into a more formal channel. The next course of action was that the alleged perpetrator would be sent a formal letter quoting the tenancy agreement and drawing their attention to the officer's power to start possession proceedings. A small number of housing officers adopted this approach in all cases so that the tenant being complained about was put on immediate notice that they could be evicted if found to be in breach of the tenancy agreement. In another study of housing disputes, Karn *et al.* (1993) found that seeking compliance with tenancy agreements was an approach commonly taken by social landlords when dealing with 'nuisance' disputes. Housing officers indicated that the majority of cases were 'resolved' at this stage.

4.21　Much discussion with mediators revolved around the problems caused by the issue of a formal letter to the party complained about outlining the council's power to evict. It was suggested during interviews that using the tenancy agreement was comparable to using a sledge hammer to crack a nut (see HO6). Social tenants are particularly vulnerable to the threat of being made homeless. Accommodation in the private sector is much more expensive than social housing and purchasing a house or flat beyond most tenants' means. In addition, there is considerable inequality of bargaining power between the tenant and the council. Tenants' identity is legally constituted and their formal obligations and responsibilities dictated by their tenancy agreement. The situation creates few incentives for tenants to contest the action taken by the council. The issuing of a formal letter threatening eviction is more realistically seen as silencing a dispute as resolving it.

4.22　There was some indication amongst residents interviewed for the study that the threat of eviction could actually exacerbate the dispute. Interviews with mediators confirmed this view. In mediators' experience, the recipient of the letter often assumed that the complainant had encouraged the council to threaten eviction. As one of the mediators commented:

> *The letter is produced to instil fear and that is what it does. Within minutes of receiving the letter the loss of home, job, children's school, child care arrangements, all flash before the person's eyes. All these thoughts go through their head. I reckon that I can always tell after a few minutes of talking to someone whether they've had a letter!*

4.23　By way of confirmation, a complainant explained what could happen from a more personal perspective:

> *Well, anyway it got into such a state that I went up and saw the housing officer about it and she said, 'I'll get in touch,' and all that. Well, it didn't do any good and eventually I had to go back up there again and I said to her, 'You'll have to do something a bit more severe to make them come round a bit 'cause they are not taking any notice.' Well, she wrote them a letter and I never got to see that letter properly. Well, anyway, I had been talking to [the respondent] the day before, and all this lark, and the morning she got it she came stomping down. Oh, she was doing her nut, 'Look what you have done to me!' and all that. I said, 'Who says I've sent the letter and all this caper, I didn't send the letter?'... And then her husband came down and he had a go at me as well and said he hoped that we would both die of cancer. (US04)*

3. Court action

4.24   Less commonly, housing officers will instigate court action to deal with a problem. Since the passing of the 1996 Housing Act, housing offices have been able to use a fast-track court system for repossessions and dealing with nuisance. Despite their scope Dignan *et al.* (1996) found in their research that statutory powers were not frequently used. Only one in 20 local authority cases reported to them were dealt with in this way and ES departments similarly only used formal measures in five per cent of their nuisance cases.[4] Interviews conducted for this study revealed that housing officers did not feel these legal remedies were always appropriate. Some did not like to threaten their tenants with eviction although one housing officer suggested that this depended on individual housing officers' attitude towards their tenants' interests and needs (HO5).

4.25   In interviews, the new fast-track system was identified as quicker, but rather cumbersome with one interviewee suggesting that injunctions can take up to two years to obtain for noise nuisance. All the housing officers in the study mentioned the amount of work involved in putting together sufficient evidence to gain an eviction. A number mention the unwillingness of the courts to evict vulnerable tenants. In the words of one housing officer: 'It is hard to evict an old lady even when she is causing a nuisance, the courts won't grant it.' It was also suggested that complainants were often unwilling to act as a witness in court and air their grievance against a neighbour in a public forum. Housing officers also complained that the evidential burden for the council remained high. As one environmental health officer in Southwark has argued:

> *The enforcement procedure for dealing with domestic complaints can be lengthy, involving officer visits, installation and analysis of recording devices, liaison with housing officers, service of Notices, compiling witness statement, court procedures for warrants and prosecutions and, ultimately, seizure of noise-making equipment. (SMC 1997, p.8)*

4.26 Elsewhere, concern has also been expressed that tenants will exploit the many technical and substantive defences available (Dignan *et al.* 1996; see also Karn *et al.* 1993).

4.27 The data presented in this chapter suggest that there is some scope for the use of mediation in resolving disputes between neighbours. A number of disputes brought to the attention of housing officers are managed rather than resolved and formal letters threatening eviction can exacerbate rather than undermine levels of conflict. Mediators in the study argued that mediation could be used to help the parties work through their grievances and provide a forum in which they could explore ways of living together more peacefully. In addition, a number of housing officers mentioned that the courts looked more favourably on eviction applications if mediation had been tried. Thus, mediation could be used to demonstrate that the housing office had taken all reasonable steps to try to resolve the problem. But, despite these suggestions, housing officers did not make extensive use of mediation. In the remainder of this chapter we explore why not.

Referring cases to mediation

4.28 As we have already suggested, housing and ES officers play a pivotal role in the referral of cases to SMC. Out of 159 cases referred to the housing project from September 1998 to August 1999 142 (89 per cent) came from housing officers.[5] Moreover, 297 (90 per cent) parties who used SMC found out about mediation through a housing officer. By way of contrast, only one per cent found out about the mediation agency through a leaflet. Similarly, 149 (83 per cent) parties referred through the Environmental Services Project had been told about SMC by an ES officer and only one (one per cent) found out about it by leaflet.[6]

4.29 SMC devotes a considerable amount of time to developing links with housing officers.[7] Despite this, it is clear that the process of building good relationships is on-going and has to be maintained if mediation is to have a profile in the borough (SMC 1997). The fact that there is often a high turnover of housing officers can generate additional work for SMC and make their task of developing trust much harder. All of the mediators interviewed endeavoured to make regular contact with housing officers. This included doing presentations for new staff, reporting the results of mediations to them and generally finding reasons to keep in touch. They also stressed that they are prepared to give advice about a case, even if it is not referred, although not many housing officers appear to opt for this service.

4.30 Data from SMC's database on 159 referrals made in one year demonstrate that there was some variation between housing officers about the sort of cases they considered suitable for mediation. Their views reflected their willingness to refer cases. Figure 4.3 shows the rate of referral from the 16 neighbourhood offices in the borough. It can be seen from this that, although all the housing offices had referred at least one case, housing staff from some offices were much more likely to use SMC's services than others. Why was this?

Figure 4.3 Number of referrals over 12-month period by neighbourhood office

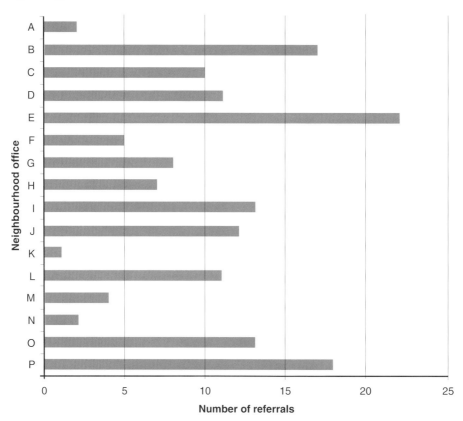

4.31 Most housing officers specified two situations in which they did not think it would be appropriate to refer to mediation. Firstly, the majority did not think it was appropriate to refer cases where there was low tolerance of the anti-social behaviour involved. Cases involving criminal activity, such as racial harassment, domestic violence or homophobic behaviour were amongst those referred to specialist units within the council or the legal department. Mediation was considered inappropriate because housing officers were not interested in encouraging the parties to find a compromise. In these cases, the tenancy agreement and power of eviction within it was most likely to be used as a first step followed by an application for an injunction to stop the behaviour being complained about. In these very serious cases, housing officers took other immediate action. Temporary accommodation might be offered to the victim at the outset or, where there was a risk of arson or retaliation, anti-incendiary post boxes might be fitted to the victim's front door. Secondly, mental health problems were also not considered suitable for mediation. A number of housing officers described the position of those responsible for anti-social behaviour as a direct result of a mental illness as having interests which were irreconcilable with those of the complainant. Mediators confirmed that these were problematic cases to handle through mediation in which it could be difficult for the parties to come to a shared understanding of the causes of the problems. Mediators and housing officers shared the view that such cases were best referred to specialists in social services.

4.32　Housing officers also identified cases which were suitable for mediation. These included:

- cases where resolution could be facilitated by mutual understanding e.g., differences in lifestyles;

- cases which could not be described as a statutory nuisance and could not be managed through legal channels;

- multi-faceted cases such as those involving children were more likely to be referred by some housing officers;

- minor incidents.

4.33　Significantly, mediation is seen as an addition to the traditional process of managing disputes rather than an alternative to it. The majority of housing officers would not consider a referral to mediation until they had exhausted all informal attempts at resolution. Only two housing officers interviewed indicated that they would consider mediation in every case. In the words of one officer: 'Mediation is an option but it is not the first option that we would consider. We look at all other options and ways of dealing with it first.'

4.34　Despite reservations about the suitability of all cases for mediation, the majority of housing officers were complimentary about the service provided by SMC. Their assessments of the agency's success rate ranged from 20-90 per cent of cases referred. A number of advantages of mediation were identified. Mediators were seen as being able to identify the underlying causes of complaints and to devote 'quality time' to resolution. It was also suggested that tenants might be prepared to be more honest with mediators than they were with housing officers. As one housing officer explained:

> *SMC have the time to get under the issues. Often, the problem is not housing related [but] relates to personal differences. Housing officers have no time to get to the bottom of the problems ... SMC tend to find the missing piece of the jigsaw that we don't get for many reasons. Maybe because it would go on their files, could result in an eviction. There are many reasons.*

4.35 In a similar vein, it was frequently suggested that mediators could perform a counselling function which helped people to come to terms with the complaint about them and its consequences. One housing officer also argued that mediation could be used as a way of educating people about different cultural attitudes and standards of behaviour. Others mentioned that SMC had been of use in identifying a past history with certain complainants. Some problematic tenants tend to move around the borough, making it difficult for officers to keep track of them. SMC can provide a cross-borough organisational memory when it has already had some involvement with a tenant.

4.36 Secondly, the majority of officers stressed the importance of SMC's independent standing and practical approach. In the words of one officer:

> *They have the culture. That is, they are independent. There isn't the bureaucracy attached to them. The tenants feel that they are being advised and helped, that the people in the centre do not have an axe to grind, that in a sense they don't really care about the dispute.*

4.37 A number of housing officers felt that as a result of their common-sensical approach, SMC was better able to manage tenants' expectations. In part, this was also attributed to the friendlier and more conciliatory environment provided by mediators.

Box 4.1: Views of mediation

'Mediation takes the housing officer out of the scene. This is very helpful.'

'Housing officers would not be able to solve the cases like SMC as they are part of the council. People can talk their heart out to others not connected to the council.'

'SMC contact the parties when the problem arises and they use a straightforward process to reach an agreement.'

4.38 Mediators were also seen to reduce the workload of housing officers. This was particularly the case with 'difficult' complaints which could not be managed through a formal letter. For most officers a referral to SMC marked the end of their involvement with the dispute. They would only become involved again if the Centre or one of the disputants contacted them directly. One other described it as, 'work off my shoulders' and a 'reprieve'. Another suggested that the intervention of SMC could provide an opportunity for officers to spend time on other disputes which they had a better chance of resolving themselves. A number of housing officers interviewed referred to the emotional strain of dealing with tenant disputes.

4.39   Some criticisms of SMC were also made by housing officers. Firstly, a number noted that they would like more feedback from mediators about the progress of cases, although the majority accepted that SMC had recently introduced new procedures and was attempting to do this. This tended not to reflect a lack of confidence in SMC's ability to do the job. As one housing officer said: 'I think the attitude was that they were doing a good job so leave them to it, which is fair enough really.' Another housing officer mentioned that this caused a problem as they could not get back to the parties until they had heard from SMC about the outcome of the case. If they got no feedback then it looked as if they were abandoning their tenants by not contacting them. Secondly, it could take a long time to get the parties to mediation and resolve the issues. A few housing officers expressed some concerns that the majority of mediators were white. They were worried that this could cause problems if the dispute had a racial or cultural element to it.

4.40   Significantly, some housing officers saw no need for mediation. It can be seen from figure 4.3 above that a handful of housing officers referred five or less cases to SMC over a 12-month period. This compares with an average of just under 10 referrals per housing officer across the borough. This group of sceptics considered that the majority of disputes could be solved by sending out a formal letter or talking the issues through with the parties. They argued that more serious disputes were often dealt with through specialist channels and this left only a very small pool of cases which could be considered for mediation.

Mediator views of referrals

4.41   How did staff at SMC feel about the incidence and timing of referrals? Mediators at SMC were concerned that housing officers were not referring enough cases to them and that there was considerable scope for an increase in the number of cases they managed on behalf of the council. Mediators were concerned that many disputes were referred too late in the process when positions had become entrenched. This caused problems as these disputes were often much more difficult to mediate. On some, very rare, occasions SMC has refused a referral because positions have become too embedded to make mediated resolution an option. SMC staff recommended that the appropriate time for a referral was when a complaint is responded to with a counter-allegation. This was considered significant as it is the point at which a grievance becomes a dispute.

4.42   Ironically, while heightening the tensions between the parties, mediators argued that they could also use formal letters threatening eviction to their advantage. By explaining to recipients that this was standard practice and not prompted by the complainant, and by explaining to the complainant what had happened, they found they could immediately quell lots of the anger which had been fuelling the parties' grievance. As one argued: 'The letter is often the crisis. Once you've got over that, you know, faced up to the worst case scenario and take the parties away from the possibility, it is easier to get them into mediation.'

4.43   Mediators recognised that there were some housing officers who had been extremely supportive of mediation. However, these remained in the minority and it was argued that some anti-mediation liaison officers were preventing colleagues from using the service. As one of the mediators argued:

> *Some housing officers act as though we are taking their cases away.*
> *I wish they wouldn't feel like that. I would like them to think of us as*
> *assisting them. After all, we can deal with the conflict but we can't take*
> *away the underlying problem. That's up to them.*

4.44   Another suggested that the position might be improved if it were disputants who made the decision to have their cases referred to mediation. It was suggested that housing officers should see it as part of their role to disseminate information about community mediation more widely so that residents could make their own choice about the process they wanted to adopt to resolve their dispute. Even supportive housing officers needed to be constantly reminded of the mediation option if they were to meet their annual quota of referrals. Interviews with housing officers confirmed the impression of SMC staff that mediators need to be proactive in encouraging referrals. As one housing officer remarked: 'SMC try to get us to keep mediation in the forefront but it doesn't always work. We tend to only refer cases when prompted. It is not necessarily the first thing that we think of.'

4.45   And, in the words of another: 'Mediation is underused. It should be a first line option but it is an afterthought at the moment. Until a mediator comes round to see us, I'm not really goaded into action.'

Conclusion

4.46   This chapter has reviewed the role of council officers in the handling of disputes and their attitude towards mediation. It has demonstrated that the majority of disputes which arise between neighbours do not come to their attention and that the formal legal powers granted to local authorities for handling neighbourhood disputes and nuisance are extensive but rarely used. The evidential burden they impose is considered weighty and formal legal tools are not always appropriate in the circumstances. However, the threat of using the powers has proven to be of great use in the management of neighbourhood disputes as most disputes appear to 'go away' once eviction has been threatened. Referral to mediation instead of this could be said to increase the cost of disputes which might otherwise go away. But the closure of cases is not the same as resolution and mediators involved in the study argue that when disputes are suppressed in this way they tend to fester and may continue to place a burden on the state through the use of other public services such as the NHS and police. Mediators at SMC work hard to encourage council officers to refer cases for mediation but it is clear that some remain sceptical about the value of mediation. Others are fearful of an overlap in jurisdiction. All require constant prompting to even consider mediation as an option on a regular basis. In the chapter which follows we will look at the characteristics of the disputes which are referred and how they are handled.

Endnotes

1. The number reflects the incidence of complaints not the number of disputes i.e. they record each complaint as a new service request.

2. Unfortunately, the noise team does not record the gender of complainants nor resolution times.

3. Where commercial operators are involved, officers follow the guidelines of the Cabinet Office Concordat (Murphy, 2000).

4. Based on data from Dignan *et al.* (1996) on action taken by environmental health officers in response to domestic noise complaints: 1982-93/4.

5. These data were drawn from SMC's database. A further one per cent heard about SMC through Environmental Services, one per cent saw SMC's leaflet and a final one per cent heard of their services through a mediator. Data were missing in a further 14 (nine per cent) instances of the 159 cases.

6. In a further 19 (21 per cent) cases the source of information was not known.

7. In addition, many officers from local police stations have received mediation awareness training and the aim is that all operational police officers from the borough would be involved in this way. The borough police liaison officer has reported that referrals to SMC are increasingly becoming the norm in civil dispute cases for the police (SMC, 1997). SMC has also reported that housing officers have more confidence in the Centre when referring cases there and that they are beginning to refer cases at an earlier stage.

Chapter 5: Disputes and their causes – Towards a politicisation of grievances

5.1 This chapter reviews the characteristics of the neighbour disputes referred to Southwark Mediation Centre (SMC) and suggests how the causes of the disputes came to be understood. It considers who becomes involved in disputes and the tendency, which SMC shares with other mediation organisations, to individualise the dispute. However, it is also suggested that the individualisation of the cause of the grievance is not complete. Housing officers and mediators demonstrated a willingness to place their explanation of the causes of disputes within a broader economic, social and political context. Rather than conceptualising disputes as arising because of low thresholds of tolerance or communication problems, interviewees suggested that many of the grievances reported arise because of environmental conditions which are common within disadvantaged inner-city boroughs.

5.2 The chapter draws on the research team's content analysis of files, a database set up and managed by staff at SMC and interviews with housing officers and disputants. The first section of this chapter provides background information about cases and reviews the incidence of referrals, the gender of the parties and the involvement of other agencies. The second section provides details of the allegations made and presents some case studies which draw on interviews with disputing neighbours and participant observations of mediation sessions.

Number of disputes handled by the mediation agency

5.3 Dignan *et al.*'s (1996) research on community mediation centres suggested that the 20 centres which responded to the survey received 2652 referrals from a range of different sources with the majority coming directly from the disputants (21 per cent), housing departments (19 per cent) Citizens Advice Bureaux and advice centres (16 per cent) and the police or probation service (12 per cent). By way of contrast, data from this study revealed that the vast majority of cases handled by SMC are referred by housing officers in accordance with the quotas agreed in service-level contracts. Data from SMC's database on 12 month's-worth of referrals show that of the 159 cases referred in 1998/9, approximately 135 (85 per cent) came from this housing officers. Other sources of referrals include police harassment teams, domestic violence units, community police officers; local doctors; businesses and housing co-operatives (SMC 1997).

> **Box 5.1: The generation gap**
>
> 'She is an old-age pensioner, I am a young mother with a family. Obviously, I have young children and we both have back gardens. When I first moved in here she used to complain that the kids used to touch her roses and to prevent this I erected a six-foot fence at my own expense. She then complained that when my son plays football, the football goes over and knocks the petals off her roses … although I apologised she kept on about the fact that the roses had been there for 26 years. So, in the end, I said enough is enough, they are roses and they will grow. I went to the council and made a formal complaint about her.'

5.4   Figure 5.1 shows new cases by year and the project they are managed under[1]. Because housing officers are limited in the number of cases they can refer to SMC by the council's contract with them, Figure 5.1 does not represent the level of demand for the mediation agency's services but the constraints on supply. The impact of this constraint can be seen in the case of Environmental Services where the number of cases opened in the last two years shown levels off around their quota of 110.

5.5   Moreover, a movement of cases away from the Housing Project can be explained by the fact that the acting co-ordinator responsible for the Housing Project was on leave.

5.6   The particularly high number of referrals which came from state officials to SMC prompts concerns of the kind discussed in Chapter Two, that the informal processes of dispute resolution offered merely provide a supplementary procedure to those of the state rather than an alternative to them. These concerns are reinforced in the present study by the fact that housing officers have admitted to using mediation only when all traditional methods for resolving the case in-house have been tried an failed. Thus, rather than taking cases out of the formal procedure, mediation is responsible for adding another layer to it. Concerns about the view of housing officers that mediation is just another method at their disposal are further reinforced by housing officers' criticisms of SMC not being sufficiently accountable to them about the progress of cases referred.

Figure 5.1 New cases by year and project

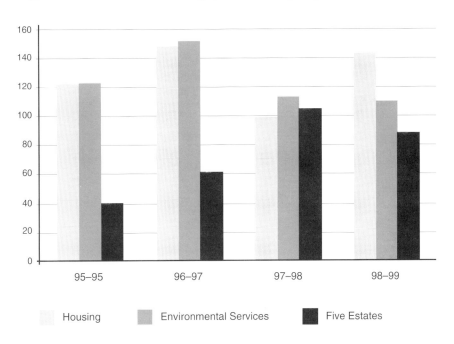

The dynamics of the dispute

5.7   Who becomes involved in neighbour disputes? Are some members of the
       population more likely to become embroiled in disputes with their neighbours
       than others? The lack of data on disputes referred to housing officers prohibits
       conclusions being drawn on the characteristics of disputes but Genn's (1999)
       recent study of the legal problems faced by a random sample of 4125 adults
       demonstrated that disputes relating to neighbours, whether experienced by
       owner occupiers or tenants differed from the dominant pattern of disputes.
       A significantly higher proportion of those experiencing problems with their
       neighbours were in the 65-years-plus age bracket, there were fewer in the 25-44
       years age bracket and women were over represented. Respondents in neighbour
       disputes were also more likely to be economically inactive and to have lower
       household incomes than was the norm for disputants.

Box 5.2: The patter of tiny feet

'It sounds a bit silly, I know, but their bedroom was above mine and, unfortunately, they hadn't got any covering on their floors so the baby used to get out of bed - it sounds a bit silly talking about a baby - used to get out of bed and pick things up and bang the floor. That went on until the early hours of the morning.'

Box 5.3: Misuse of overflow pipe

'We have a patio ... and they have a balcony upstairs with an overflow. That overflow is there for heavy rain [and] that type of thing, not tipping water [and bleach] down which she was doing ... I had the windows open and I had pretty good curtains up and the water came in and flooded us ... That kept on quite a few times and we had an argument and I thought, I can't take this because I have ill health, you know.'

5.8   Data collected for the present study on the characteristics of cases referred to mediation show that women complainants (56 per cent) were also more likely to have their disputes with their neighbours referred to SMC than were men (29 per cent)[3]. This finding reflects Rothschild's (1996) contention that 58 per cent of complainants in her intensive case study of the San Francisco Community Board were women, 33 per cent were men and 10 per cent couples. Moreover, 48 per cent of respondents in cases referred to SMC were women, making them three times as likely to have complaints made about them referred to the agency than men (16 per cent)[4]. Analysis of data held by SMC on 151 cases received by the from 1997/8 reveals that the largest proportion of disputes involved a complaint by one woman about another (42 per cent). These data are presented in table 5.1.

Table 5.1 Gendered dynamics of disputes referred to mediation agency (n=151)*

Gender of complainants	Gender of respondents			
	Male	**Female**	**Mixed couple**	**Mixed group**
Male	11 (7%)	25 (17%)	3 (2%)	4 (3%)
Female	20 (13%)	64 (42%)	5 (3%)	3 (2%)
Mixed couple	1 (1%)	9 (6%)	6 (4%)	1 (1%)
Mixed group	0	1 (1%)	0	2 (1%)

* These data were missing or not applicable in 56 cases.

5.9 How are these data to be interpreted? Without the aid of baseline data on all disputes which arise between neighbours in the community with which to compare these data it is impossible to know whether there are more female disputants in Southwark or whether it is housing officers propensity to refer disputes involving women which account for these trends. Data reported by Genn (1999) at national level suggest that the former explanation is most likely to account for the data. Census data reveal that women in the borough are more likely to be unemployed or economically inactive than men and as a result are more exposed to neighbours and problems with their immediate environment. It has also been argued in previous research that women are more likely to enter into a dispute when it involves someone for whom they have a caring responsibility, such as children, the elderly or infirm (Lloyd-Bostock and Mulcahy 1994; Allsop 1994). Moreover, the data on referrals to SMC may also suggest that women may be more predisposed to conciliatory resolution than men. In her seminal work on women and family mediation, Grillo (1991) has opined that mediation may be a more natural choice for women, but not because women necessarily prefer to be conciliatory. Rather, she argues that there is a pervasive societal prohibition on female anger in Western culture which makes it more likely that disputes involving women will be encouraged to try mediation with its emphasis on conflict as counterproductive.

Who gets involved in disputes?

5.10 Commentators have argued that there is a trend for formalised Anglo-American dispute resolution models to individualise disputes and to construe them as adversarial encounters between two parties (Damaska 1986). In contrast, socio-legal researchers have often placed emphasis on the group dynamics of disputes. In their impressive review of third-party roles in disputes, Black and Baumgartner (1983) pay attention to a range of roles performed by third parties from the gossip and go-between to adviser, advocate and champion. In a similar vein, Mather and Yngvesson (1980-1) have stressed the importance of groups and social networks in narrowing or expanding the issues at stake between disputants.

Table 5.2 Classifications of disputing parties (n = 155)*

	Individual	Household	Group
Individual	113 (73%)	22 (14%)	11 (7%)
Household		7 (4%)	1 (1%)
Group			1 (1%)

* 51cases were classified as other or missing

5.11   In their discussion of the conflict resolution activity of the San Francisco Community Boards, Du Bow and McEwen (1996) describe how mediators in the programme resisted the tendency to individualise conflict by permitting and encouraging couples, groups and neighbours to bring the collective concerns to mediation. In this way, they argue that the Board acknowledged the complexity of neighbourhood conflicts and was responsive to the ways in which the parties understood and defined the issues. However, a review of the literature on community mediation programmes suggests that such practice is the exception rather than the norm. In this study, it appeared from SMC files that 73 per cent of disputes involved two individual disputants. Table 5.2 shows the breakdown of these and other cases.

> **Box 5.4: The deaf old lady**
>
> 'We had problems with a 90-year-old woman opposite. She would do things like, about 4am in the morning, turn on Radio 5 Live full blast. She would bang on her ceiling with her walking stick. We would constantly hear her on the telephone telling lies about us. She was quite deaf and didn't wear a hearing aid and the property wasn't sound-proofed at the time.'

5.12   However, interviews with housing officers and mediators have suggested that these data reflect recording practice[5] rather than an adequate picture of who is involved in neighbour disputes in Southwark. This contention is supported by the fact that other parties were often present on visits to the disputants' homes made by mediators. Moreover, the dissatisfaction of other local residents about the respondent's or complainant's behaviour was often reported on such occasions. It is also clear that other parties may have become involved in the processing of the dispute before it is referred to SMC. Our analysis of the 207 SMC case files received between 1 April 1997 and 31 March 1998 demonstrated that organisations such as the police, housing trusts, health workers or social workers were also involved in disputes referred to SMC. These agencies had some involvement prior to, or in parallel with, the mediation agency in at least 14 per cent of the cases referred to them.

5.13 Statistical returns to funding bodies also indicate that a number of cases are eventually processed by other agencies at the instigation of SMC. After a preliminary perusal of the case, mediators sometimes felt that their involvement in a case was inappropriate and that another agency was better suited to deal with the matter. Examples include referrals back to the housing officer where eviction proceedings had been started; criminal charges were being pursued against one of the parties; and cases where social services needed to provide specialist help to deal with underlying problems. However, it was clear that mediators were increasingly disposed towards retaining cases referred to them. It can be seen from figure 5.2 that between 1995 and 1999 the percentage of closed cases that are processed elsewhere has decreased from 34 per cent to 13 per cent in 1998/9.

Figure 5.2 Number of closed cases referred on by SMC

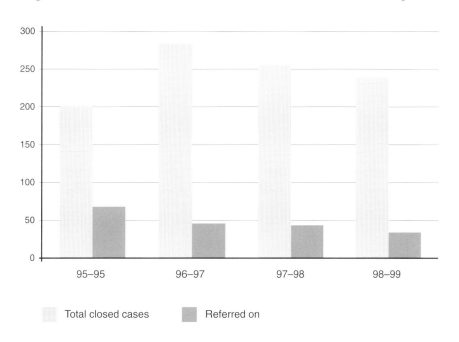

What do disputants complain about?

5.14 Dignan *et al.* (1996) have argued that 42 per cent of disputes between neighbours involved noise, followed by family/relationship disputes (11 per cent) and abusive behaviour (9 per cent) (see also Brown and Marriot, 1993). In the current study, the problems caused by noise in the borough have been recognised by the Local Health Authority (Lambeth, Southwark and Lewisham Health Authority 1997). In its 1996/7 annual report, the health authority acknowledged that so-called neighbour noise causes anxiety, stress and interrupted sleep which is identified as posing a threat to public health. It was estimated that 80 per cent of complaints directed to the Environmental Health Department at Southwark concerned noise. At SMC, a total of 313 allegations were made in the 195[6] cases that were received by SMC between 1 April 1997 and 31 March 1998. Between one and five allegations were recorded for each dispute and the average was 1.6 per case. There were 91 cases where the agency had successfully made contact with both the complainant and respondent and both sides of the dispute have been heard and recorded. In these cases, the number of allegations increased to 1.9 per case. The allegations made in those cases where contact had been made with both parties are listed in table 5.3. These data suggest that a higher proportion (52 per cent) of cases in Southwark involve noise. This may be explained by the large amount of high density accommodation in the borough. Further analysis of the 207 cases

Table 5.3 Allegations made in 91 cases in which the agency made contact with both the complainant and the respondent

Allegation made	No. of times cited		No. of cases cited	
Normal noise e.g. footsteps, children playing, use of utilities	55	(23%)	49	(29%)
Abnormal noise e.g. amplified music, parties	38	(22%)	38	(23%)
Abuse e.g. verbal name calling, spreading rumours and lies	24	(14%)	20	(12%)
Property, rubbish and hygiene e.g. blocking communal areas, urinating in lift, car parking	24	(14%)	17	(10%)
Race e.g. discrimination, racial abuse	7	(4%)	5	(3%)
Animals e.g. dog scratching, barking	5	(3%)	6	(4%)
Assault e.g. physical violence*	4	(2%)	3	(2%)
Other e.g. possession of firearm, coming to door in underpants, cooking smells, religion, council	15	(9%)	31	(18%)
Total	**172**	**(100%)**	**169**	**(101%)**

*   SMC data on 159 referrals in a 12-month period confirm that there are only a small number of cases where violence is threatened (6) or has occurred (14). This is probably because these cases are filtered out for referrals and sent instead to the police (see chapter four).

†   More than one allegation could be made per case

received in one year revealed that in 75 per cent of all cases at least one allegation related to a form of noise, whether normal or abnormal. Box 5.7 highlights that there was a vast range of noise allegations cited in the cases analysed. The type of allegations cited also draws attention to problems of poor insulation in many Southwark homes.

Box 5.5: Dirty linen in public

'Her daughter … I'm not being nasty, ok, but when she was like on her period, she used to throw all her dirty tampons with her knickers and things like that in my front garden and a lot of things were happening … My house got raided and it was to do with [her]. She told them I was a big time drug dealer and there was lots of police at my house … when they didn't find nothing they told me it was her.'

5.15 It is clear that the range of allegations and their severity varies considerably from complaints about normal domestic noise to feuds which involve racial harassment and the police. Boxes 5.1-5.7 give examples of the range of grievances which emerge. Interviews with disputants who had used the services of SMC revealed that the allegations made may increase as grievances escalate. A good example is the account of a dispute given in Box 5.6. The feud described developed further over time and involved the regular obstruction of the interviewees' driveway, the insertion of superglue into all their external locks and a visit by a bogus policeman.

Box 5.6: Rites of passage

'Well, it originally started with the next-door mother dying and I was out the front working on a car the day of the funeral and didn't know the funeral cortege was going to go down through the street … It never dawned on me it was her mother and, in the evening, my wife went in there to talk to her and [they] wanted to know why I had turned my back on the grandmother. All hell broke loose from that moment … Then he [her boyfriend] parked his van half-way across the entrance to my drive-in and I put a note in a plastic bag, 'cos it was pouring down with rain, under his windscreen asking him to keep clear of the entrance. The next morning it was under the windscreen wipers of my little van and written across it in big bold letters was "bollocks", and from then on it was war.'

Box 5.7: Examples of noise allegations

- Fish tank vibrating
- Fridge opening
- Toilet flushing
- Love-making
- Light switches going on and off
- Parties and loud stereos
- Televisions
- Use of stairs
- Coffee cups being put on uncarpeted floors
- Quarrels
- Children playing
- Workers returning from night shift

External causes of neighbourhood disputes

5.16 Some critics of community mediation projects have expressed concerns about the failure of mediation to link individual concerns with wider political issues (see, for instance, the essays in Engle-Merry and Milner 1996). In part, this failure can be attributed to the process of perceiving disputes as occurring between individuals rather than groups But it can also be linked to the tendency to view the causes of the dispute as coming about as a result of the activity of the individuals involved. Rothschild (1996), for example, has argued that disputes are commonly rephrased as interpersonal problems of communication. In turn, this is seen as encouraging mediators to direct attention to the relational and emotional aspect of conflicts.

5.17 An important finding of the present research was the way in which mediators attributed disputes to underlying conditions of life in Southwark as much as to personality traits of individuals involved or unreasonable behaviour. In the course of interviews with mediators and housing officers several examples of the externalisation of the causes of disputes became apparent. These data go some way to addressing the concerns of critics that mediation inevitably involved the de-politicisation of disputes. Attention was paid to three particular factors which helped set the scene for conflict. Firstly, frequent reference was made to the stresses of inner-city living. A much higher proportion of residents in Southwark are social tenants and few have the resources to move elsewhere. Interviews cited the high incidence of unemployment, high-density living, noise and pollution as factors to take into account when trying to understand disputing dynamics. These could make living conditions in the borough very stressful and affect thresholds of tolerance.

5.18 It was also argued that properties available to tenants were often unsuitable for multiple occupancy. For example, some areas in the borough have a high number of conversion properties. These are commonly Victorian houses which have been converted into flats. Problems arose with noise because they had not been designed for the number of people who now live in them and insulation was often poor. A number of interviewees mentioned that there were not enough places for children to play in on local estates and that their noise often upset other residents, especially the elderly. One housing officer indicated that, even where there were large recreational spaces, parents often felt uncomfortable letting their children play in them. He gave the example of a local park which parents avoided because it tended to be used by drunks and drug addicts who left bottles and syringes lying around. There were also concerns that properties were often badly allocated or designed. As one mediator explained: 'The design of properties is a problem. They tend to put small units underneath family accommodation, therefore creating problems. This is not taken into consideration when building new properties.' Analysis of 207 SMC case files suggested that high-density living is a factor in prompting conflict. The majority of the disputes (68 per cent) were between neighbours in the same housing unit, such as a block of flats or maisonettes. A further 30 per cent of neighbours lived in the same road or estate. Environmental Services have also confirmed that their impression is that most complaints about noise are between immediate neighbours.

5.19 Secondly, it was argued that some disputes should be understood as reflecting a clash of cultures. Interviewees argued that some groups were intolerant of one another because of different perceptions of what constituted acceptable behaviour. Instances of this included inter-generational disputes; conflicts over different life-styles; inter-cultural disputes and disputes between homosexual and heterosexual individuals and groups. Commenting on inter-racial tensions, one housing officer argued:

> *A lot of problems revolve around cultural mix and the different ways of living people have. We haven't learnt to live together yet. There is a need for more tolerance and tolerance takes years to become embedded. When an African family celebrate a child's birthday, the whole family come round and we party and make noise! White people have a short tea for just children. We haven't found the balance yet between these different ways. No one has come up with rules about what is acceptable.*

5.20 Finally, a number of interviewees also drew attention to the high incidence of mental health problems and the impact of this on 'disputes'. Not all housing officers had the same experience of tenants with mental health problems but, those that did argued that illnesses of this kind could precipitate unpredictable and unsociable behaviour. They contended that the real problem arose because other members of the community amongst whom the mentally ill lived did not always understand their behaviour and needs. Even where they did, they admitted that behaviour associated with such illness could prove stressful when living in close proximity to it. One housing officer estimated that as many as 60 or 70 per cent of her cases were caused or exacerbated by a mental health problem. In the words of another: 'These cases aren't disputes as such. Although mental health problems are the least in number, they can cause the most problems. In some cases the tenant has burnt their own home down and broken into their own flat.'

5.21 The problems faced by the mentally ill were exacerbated by a lack of co-ordination between local agencies. Several housing officers mentioned that they did not feel that social services were as helpful as they should be in accepting responsibility for such clients. Co-ordination between public sector service providers with a responsibility for this client group could also be made difficult by the fact that the council was not routinely provided with any information about tenants with mental health concerns until there is a problem. This meant that housing officers could not plan in advance or be alerted to potential problems. In the words of one officer:

> *We can use the mental health unit but this is a very long process. The problem is finding someone in the mental health network that knows the tenant that you have. Most of them will only know where their patients or clients are if they have a serious problem. (HO3)*

5.22 The only formal legal process for dealing with such problems was the use of eviction. Housing officers were concerned that this was inappropriate for this client group made up of individuals who needed support and help.

Conclusion

5.23 This chapter has presented data on the characteristics of disputes referred to SMC. The number of cases referred to SMC is governed more by the quotas imposed on referrals than demand. It is clear that certain types of residents are more likely to have their dispute referred to mediation, most notably women. But when ascertaining who is involved in the dispute official statistics do not reflect the whole story. Networks of family, friends and other neighbours may also have become embroiled in the conflict although records rarely reflect this. Certain types of disputes are also likely to be referred with noise being the most obvious example. The chapter has emphasised that disputes between neighbours involve a wide range of issues but that most involve some form of noise allegation.

5.24 One of the most interesting findings reported in this chapter is the way in which mediators and housing officers often referred to the external causes of disputes. This shifts the emphasis away from the individualisation of blame and management of disputes as discrete activities towards the attribution of responsibility to more pervasive conditions many of which, such as poor insulation and overcrowding, are associated with urban deprivation. This theme will be pursued in chapter 8 where we will consider the concerns of critics that mediators are lackeys of the local council.

Endnotes

1. Because the Five Estates project is area-specific rather than agency specific, i.e. referrals come from a number of agencies within a geographical area, it can be difficult to separate out the cases that are managed under this project from those managed under the housing and ES projects. A dispute referred to the mediation agency by Environmental Services may be included in the statistics for the Five Estates Project as well. The Five Estates Project also differs from the other projects because the funding body does not require such detailed annual statistical reports. For this reason, some of the annual trends presented in figure 5.1 have been estimated. The annual figures for the Five Estates project are estimates based on 30 months of data.

2. A period of major re-structuring of the way in which the centre was managed during the period 1997-98 would seem to be responsible for the drop in housing project cases opened during that period.

3. A further 10 per cent of referrals came from a man and a woman and four per cent of case files had no data on the gender of the disputants involved.

4. Referrals relating to a male and female respondent accounted for a further seven per cent of cases and data were missing in 29 per cent of case files.

5. Housing officers and mediators argued that the picture presented by the data is easily explained by reference to the bureaucratic constraints on recording information about cases. Although it may become obvious in the course of processing the dispute that a number of other parties are involved neither the housing officer or mediator are empowered to talk to other parties about the dispute until they make their own complaint to the council. Moreover, mediators made clear that they prefer not to know much about the history of a case. Consequently, they do not prompt housing officers to supply many details on their referral forms so that they can approach the case 'blind'. Murray, Rau and Sherman (1989) identify this as a characteristic of many community mediation schemes.

6. The allegations made in 12 of the 207 cases analysed were missing, therefore n = 195.

Chapter 6: The processing of disputes at Southwark Mediation Centre

Introduction

6.1   This chapter considers what happens to neighbour disputes once they are referred to Southwark Mediation Centre (SMC). The emphasis is on mapping out the various routes that may be used to process disputes and on identifying levels of contact between mediators and disputants. We show that, despite the preponderance of literature which focuses on face-to-face mediation, this form of resolution remains relatively unusual in Southwark. Another key finding of the research has been that it is not always appropriate to think of successful outcomes in terms of agreements reached through mediation. Mediators' involvement in disputes may not lead to a formal settlement of the issues, but it may facilitate a clarification of issues or abandonment. These findings have implications for the way in which we determine what constitutes a successful outcome of mediators' intervention in disputes.

6.2   The chapter is in three sections. In the first part, the 'end points' of dispute processing are identified. In the second part, consideration is given to the unseen workload of mediators; the levels of intervention in those cases which do not reach settlement. The third section considers mediators' preference for shuttle mediation over face-to-face models. In the next chapter, we develop some of these themes by going on to consider the more qualitative aspects of dispute management at the Centre.

What happens to disputes referred to SMC?

6.3   Discussion of mediation amongst practitioners and academics often assumes a dominant image of mediation as a face-to-face encounter between disputants which is facilitated or moderated by one or two mediators and this is a common image across subject areas.[1] It follows from this that the success of mediation is often judged by mediators' ability to reach some form of settlement as a result of this process. Although proponents draw attention to the process benefits of mediation and its long term effects on relationships, most emphasis continues to be placed on immediate outcomes. Bush and Folger (1994) argue that despite the presence of a number of different approaches to mediation, a growing body of research tells us that a dominant pattern of practice has emerged which focuses on solving problems and getting settlements. They have suggested that this poses a problem because it gives little attention to the medium or long-term benefits of mediation as facilitating coalition building or transforming disputants through empowerment and recognition, They argue that these outcomes can be achieved even when immediate settlement cannot.

6.4   In line with this settlement approach the returns which SMC are required to submit to their funding bodies on a quarterly basis only record the progress of cases by reference to different forms of closure of cases referred. Despite this, our research suggests that the classification of closure is more complex and goes some way to identifying a broader range of processes and outcomes. There are three reasons for this:

- Firstly, that discrete episodes of face-to-face mediation occur relatively infrequently. Encounters between disputants and mediators may be drawn out over time.

- Secondly, many cases referred were not ripe for settlement or attempts at mediation.

- Finally, mediators aided the settlement of disputes in a number of other ways which did not fall within the ambit of the label of 'mediation'.

6.5   Quarterly returns provide a starting point for understanding the different routes which disputes referred to SMC can take and suggest, somewhat surprisingly, that the majority of cases referred to SMC are not mediated. Figure 6.1 shows a breakdown of the outcome of cases for the Housing Project and Environmental Services between 1995-1999.

6.6   It can be seen from these data that over half the cases referred to SMC for the housing and Environmental Services Projects are resolved or abandoned without mediation even being attempted. Less than a third of cases are resolved through shuttle or face-to-face mediation. The relatively low use of mediation is supported by other data from the study. The research team's analysis of one year's-worth of cases files (168^2) at SMC demonstrated formal written or oral agreements were generated in just 16 per cent of cases received. In the same dataset, of the cases referred to the Centre 53 (32 per cent) cases were mediated. Twenty (12 per cent) of these mediations were conducted face to face and 33 involved the mediators shuttling between the parties (20 per cent). Case files provided little data on the characteristics of cases referred to the Centre but the data available suggest that cases involving physical or verbal abuse are more likely to reach shuttle or face-to-face mediation and that cases involving abnormal noise were more likely than others to be resolved or abandoned.

Figure 6.1 Closure of cases 1995-99 Housing and ES (n=977)

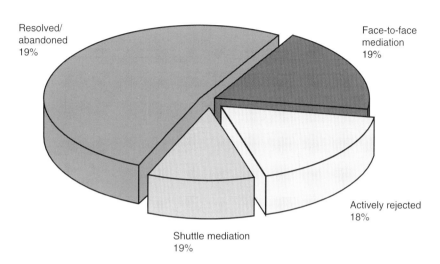

Resolved/abandoned 19%

Face-to-face mediation 19%

Actively rejected 18%

Shuttle mediation 19%

In interviews, mediators argued that, where the dispute involved inter-personal problems it was thought to be particularly helpful to use face-to-face mediation because the parties were best placed to describe their emotions and it was often important for them to experience apologies and explanation.

6.7 What happens to the cases which are not mediated? Our analysis suggests that the management of cases fell into three main categories other than shuttle or face-to-face mediation:[3]

- There was a cluster of cases in which SMC had contacted at least one of the parties but had received *no response* from the disputants.

- In a second category, SMC had made contact with at least one of the parties but the problem being complained about had either been *resolved* or the complainant wanted to *abandon* their case. In these situations mediation was rejected by default.

- In a final category, mediation was actively *rejected* as an option by the parties or mediators. This may have been because mediation was not wanted, the case was not considered suitable for mediation or SMC had decided to refer it to another agency more skilled in dealing with the issues.

6.8 Using data collected from the content analysis of one year's-worth of files figure 6.2 shows these various stages in diagrammatic form and indicates the number of cases which reached each stage. The data demonstrate SMC mediators do not get the opportunity to try mediation in over half of the cases (55 per cent) referred either because parties refuse to engage with them by not responding to their phone calls and letters or because, by the time mediators make contact, the disputants have resolved or abandoned the cases. In addition, it would seem that mediation is actively rejected by between 13 per cent (figure 6.2) and 18 per cent (figure 6.1) of cases. The high rate of non-response and abandonment suggested by the data also support the argument made in previous chapters that pursuit of complaints through formal channels is a relatively atypical response to a dispute with a neighbour.

Figure 6.2 Process used to manage neighbourhood disputes over one year (n=168)

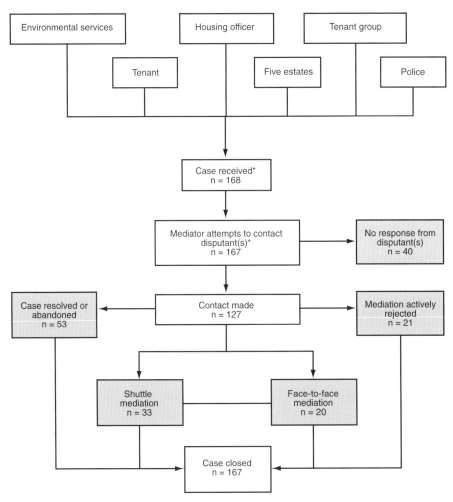

* These data are gleaned from our contact analysis of 207 files. There were five case which were on-going and data on case management was missing in another 34 cases.
** There was one case where SMC did not make contact.

6.9 The rejection of mediation as an option by disputants can be attributed to one of a number of factors. Some of these relate to the timing of referrals. In the last chapter, we reported that mediators felt that housing officers often referred cases for mediation too late when the positions of the disputants had become too entrenched. It was also clear from interviews that, while some housing officers gain the parties' agreement to send the case to SMC before referring it, other officers expect SMC to broker agreement to mediation. Although mediators felt that they were likely to have more success in encouraging the parties to try mediation than housing officers, a certain level of rejection was to be anticipated since disputants are being presented with the idea for the first time when contacted by SMC staff.

6.10 Interviewees also accepted that some disputants did not like the idea of mediation. One SMC mediator felt this had a lot to do with misunderstandings about the process and the perception that it focused on the parties becoming friends. She reflected the views of all mediators at the Centre when she said:

> *People just sort of assume that you are trying to make them all holy and that if they go to mediation then they have to become friends. One of the first things we try to get across when we talk to them is that we are not going to insult their intelligence by asking them to become buddies. What we want to achieve is a way of them living close by to each other without things being too unpleasant. When you say that you see a big look of relief on their face.*

6.11 Housing officers confirmed that some clients were wary of the notion of mediation and tended to place emphasis on the fact that many felt uncomfortable about having to engage with the other party to resolve the dispute. Others felt that some tenants did not want to transfer their problems into an arena where they might feel exposed.

The unseen workload

6.12 A major finding of the study is that mediators undertake much informal work on disputes which is not reflected in the data on outcomes presented above. A considerable amount of time and effort goes into resolving cases at each of the end points identified earlier in the chapter (see figure 6.2) Prolonged effort was not limited to those cases ending in shuttle or face-to face-mediation and resources were expended on attempts to engage with the parties whatever the outcome.

6.13 The first stage in processing all disputes was making contact with the parties. This was attempted with 99 per cent (183) of complainants[4] and 68 per cent (127) of respondents in the cases that were referred to SMC from 1 April 1997 – 31 March 1998. Contact with both the complainant and the respondent was made in 91 cases[5]. Table 6.1 gives details of the cases in which at least one attempt was made to contact the complainant or respondent by telephone, a home visit or letter.

Table 6.1 Type and frequency of contact with complainants and respondents*

	Complainant†			Respondent		
	Total contacts	Range	Average per case	Total contacts	Range	Average per case
Telephone call	199	1-10	1.1	82	1-5	0.6
Visit	126	1-10	0.7	72	1-5	0.6
Letter	153	1-6	0.8	246	1-8	1.9

* Cases were not included where no attempts at contact with the party had been made.

† Although contact with parties other than those acting as principals in the dispute was plotted it was rare for SMC to call on them.

6.14 It can be seen from the data in table 6.1 that repeated attempts are made to make initial contact. The vast majority of complainants were likely to receive a telephone call, a visit and a letter during attempts at resolution of their dispute by SMC mediators. The data also show that mediators' preferred method of contact varied according to whether staff were dealing with the complainant or the respondent. They were twice as likely to make contact with the complainant over the telephone than with the respondent. The preferred mode of contact with the respondent was in written form and mediators were twice as likely to attempt contact this way with the respondent than the complainant.

6.15 Interviews revealed that mediators are less likely to contact the respondent for a number of reasons. If the complainant did not respond to mediators' attempts to contact them then it was harder to progress with resolution. It is the complainant who fuels a formal complaint and there is little incentive for respondents to engage in attempts at resolution if the complainant appears to have abandoned their desire to pursue their grievance. It may also become clear on contacting the complainant that the dispute has been resolved between the parties, a factor which may obviate the need to contact the respondent at all.

6.16 In support of the argument that a large amount of work is put into cases which do not reach mediation figure 6.3 shows the level of activity with complainants by the outcome reached. This demonstrates that almost as many visits were made with those complainants who abandoned their case (33) as those complainants who resolved their dispute through shuttle mediation (36).

Figure 6.3 Level of activity with complainant (n=478*)

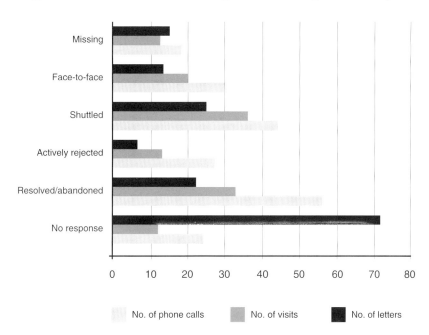

6.17 It is also clear from figure 6.3 that letter-writing activity and phone calls in cases where there is no response or the case is abandoned can actually exceed activity in mediated cases. Further analysis suggests that overall almost as many attempts to contact the complainant were made with those that didn't respond (2.8) as those that were mediated face-to-face (3.2) or shuttle mediated (3.2).

6.18 Some of these trends are also reflected in the level of contact made with respondents. Figure 6.4 shows the levels of activity with respondents.

6.19 Home visits occurred in the majority of cases where mediation was not actively rejected, or the dispute abandoned. Visits were paid to roughly half the complainants whose case had been referred to SMC. In some situations where there had been no response from disputants to initial attempts at contact, SMC mediators wrote a letter to say they would call in on a particular day in the hope that the disputant would seem them. Such 'cold calling' could often result in failure as the parties might not be at home. Our experience of attending such visits was that about 25 per cent would have to be abandoned as a result. Despite this, mediators would often continue to make attempts to engage with the parties.

Figure 6.4 Level of activity with respondent (n=400*)

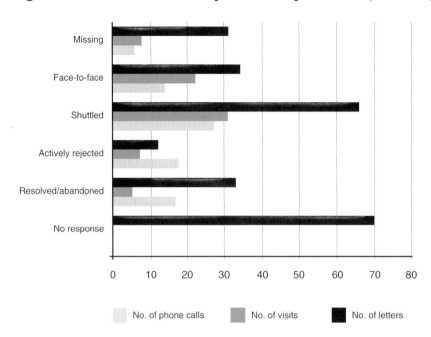

Conclusion

6.20 Socio-legal scholars have often placed emphasis on the need to look at the emergence and transformation of disputes rather than concentrate on outcomes and settlement alone. The strength of this approach is demonstrated by the data presented in this chapter which show that the agencies 'capture' of cases referred to them is low. Research participants have suggested that this is explained by two factors. Either the disputants are not attracted by the idea of mediation or disputes are referred too late when the parties have already become too entrenched. For the majority of cases referred to SMC mediation is not undertaken. The finding is important both because the empirical study allows such low take-up of mediation to be placed in context, but also because it confirms the findings of a number of other studies of mediation which demonstrate that, unless made compulsory, it is not a preferred method of dispute resolution (see, for instance, Mulcahy *et al.* 2000; Genn 1998). In this chapter we have commented on the 21 (13 per cent) cases in which mediation has been actively rejected, but passive rejection may also have occurred in the 53 (32 per cent) cases where the case was resolved or abandoned by the time initial contact was made with one of the parties, or the 40 (24 per cent) cases where there was no response from disputants. It would seem that in a total of 114 (68 per cent) cases at least one of the disputants was not interested in using the services of SMC to help resolve the dispute.

6.21   What conclusions can be drawn from this? It may be, as other studies have suggested, that whilst providing an additional 'tool' in a dispute resolution 'toolkit' that mediation is not the panacea for all dispute resolution ills that many mediation gurus would have us think. But the data also suggest that housing officers may need to be made more sensitive to the dangers of referring cases which are less ripe for mediation if the process is to be given its best chance. A final perspective from which to view the data might be to suggest that, if one of the roles ascribed to mediators by the council is to be a broker between the parties to explore whether mediation is an option, then it is inevitable that a smaller proportion of disputes will progress to mediation.

6.22   The data also demonstrate that the emphasis on mediation as a face-to-face activity is inappropriate. Face-to-face mediation is the least likely outcome of the five major outcomes identified in this chapter. Despite this, discussion of face-to-face mediation continues to dominate academic and practitioners' commentaries on mediation. When mediation becomes an option it is shuttle mediation which is the preferred form and the reasons for this are further explored in the next chapter.

6.23   The data presented draw attention to the high level of unseen work undertaken by mediators in processing cases. The amount of work they undertake on cases does not necessarily increase as they move towards shuttle or face-to-face mediation. In fact, the incidence of contact with the parties may be higher where mediation is not pursued. These data suggest that assessing the success of SMC's intervention by reference to settled cases alone is inappropriate and that the quarterly returns that they produce for some of their funding bodies can be misleading indicators of performance. This finding also has implications for costing the services of SMC as costs have to be spread across all cases and not just those which are mediated. In the next chapter we consider some of the more qualitative aspects of our evaluation of the services provided by SMC and details of how shuttle mediation is organised. The data presented are complementary to those given in this chapter as they help to explain the levels of activity and the benefits of understanding why so much effort is made to process all cases and not just those which are ripe for mediation.

Endnotes

1.   See, for example 'The sensitive bully' in Bush and Folger (1994) p. 5; 'The case of the adjacent gardens' in Felstiner and Williams (1978); Engle Merry and Milner (1995); and Mulcahy *et al.* (2000).

2. There were 207 cases which fell within the 12-month period selected for analysis but only 168 yielded sufficient data to be of use in this study.

3. In addition, there was one case in which SMC had made no contact with either of the disputants.

4. Twenty-three cases missing or not included (on-going), therefore n = 184.

5. Includes five cases that are on-going.

Chapter 7: A description of the mediation process

Introduction

7.1 This chapter describes the process of mediation as practised by mediators at Southwark Mediation Centre (SMC). It draws on participant observations of shuttle and face-to-face mediations as well as interviews with clients who have used SMC services and reviews how mediators go about the job of handling disputes and the skills they bring to bear in facilitating discussion and agreements. The chapter is deliberately descriptive rather than analytical. The story of mediation process it tells is one which will be familiar to practitioners and researchers in the field. It has already been noted that a number of different mediation models exist and that each can be seen as reflecting a number of different ideological concerns. In practice, the models tend to overlap and there are aspects of process which are common to most. The function of the chapter is to provide baseline information about process for those unfamiliar with mediation. Subsequent chapters go on to discuss the extent to which the processes described here fully reflect what occurs in mediation.

7.2 It is clear from the data presented in this chapter and previous ones that the role of mediator is a fluid one. Mediators have less formal control over their client group than do other third parties such as arbitrators or judges. Disputants may feel pressurised to try mediation in an attempt to present themselves as 'reasonable' tenants, although technically the process remains voluntary. This is significant as it means that the parties can abandon the process at any stage without financial penalties. It was shown in the last chapter that a high proportion of clients exercise this option by failing to respond to SMC's communication or by abandoning their claim. This emphasis on party autonomy is a central tenet of the philosophy of the community mediation movement.

7.3 Whether disputes reach face-to-face mediation or are abandoned, mediators have an important part to play in the identification of issues, common ground and resolution options. These alone could amount to an important outcome if they allow the dispute to evolve and facilitate the parties opening bi-lateral negotiations. Alternatively, they may decide that their grievance does not have as strong a foundation as they thought and abandon their claims or defences. This chapter focuses on all aspects of the work that mediators do with disputants and the visits they undertake. It then goes on to consider the techniques they use. In this way, the chapter hopes to demonstrate that there are a variety of outcomes to be achieved by mediation other than formal agreements.

The mediation process

7.4 It was argued in chapter two that the mediation process is generally seen as a flexible one. For this reason, it can be difficult to identify fixed stages or phases. The problem is compounded by the fact that disputants can exit the process at any time and because there are various outcomes to the dispute. However, most mediators attempted to make initial contact with the parties by telephone. Whilst the less experienced mediators were more wary of attempting in-depth discussions on the phone, all mediators nonetheless used such preliminary conversations to establish the essence of the issues in dispute and the circumstances in which the dispute had arisen. In some cases, the dispute was not pursued beyond the initial phone conversation, although there was an expectation amongst mediators that once engagement of this kind had occurred it would be followed by a home visit.[1]

> **Box 7.1: Description of role and establishing credibility**
>
> 'Southwark have been forward thinking in respect that they now see that disputes benefit from neutral third parties. We have been working with the council for around six to seven years. We know most of the area and have dealt with most difficulties between neighbours.'

Shuttle mediation

7.5 Home visits to the parties were the first stage in the process of shuttling between the disputants in an attempt at resolution. Recent research by Dignan *et al.* (1996) suggests that, despite the popular perception of mediation involving a discrete face-to-face event, shuttle mediation is now the most popular form of mediation used by community agencies in the UK. Despite this, where shuttle mediation has been debated it has often been seen as an offshoot of face-to-face mediation in which the parties break from a joint meeting to move into caucuses. Commentaries on shuttle mediation suggest that its primary purpose is for the mediator to obtain some movement away from the entrenched positions of the disputants towards settling the conflict (Odom 1986). Mediators in the study were also aware that there was not universal approval of the shuttle technique and were keen to justify their use of it. One mediator explained: 'We do lots of shuttle. I know that some mediators say that shuttle doesn't work but they are not right. Some mediators can be so blinkered. They need to get flexible.'

7.6   Observations by the research team revealed that shuttle mediation is a term which can be used to cover one of three processes at SMC: initial conversations with the parties on the phone; visits to each of the parties in their home; and separation of the parties and shuttling between them as part of a face-to-face mediation session.

7.7   Staff at the centre justified the use of shuttling on five grounds and were keen to promote the uses of shuttle mediation which was conducted over a number of weeks and in the parties' homes. Firstly, they argued that some parties were simply not prepared to engage with the other side in a face-to-face setting. In these circumstances shuttling provided a way of helping to resolve the dispute which would not be possible if only face-to-face mediation was on offer. One mediator explained how meetings could be abused by the parties: 'Some people don't want face-to-face and sometimes I am dubious [about them meeting] if they just want to settle a score in person and that can get abusive.'

7.8   She went on to suggest that their emphasis on spending time with individual disputants allowed mediators to concentrate on an exploration of the strength of their case and the feelings it aroused:

> *There are things you can do in shuttle which are not possible in face-to-face. You can challenge their account without causing them loss of face. For instance, I might say 'Now, when you say you went down and knocked on their door in all honesty was that a tap or a bang?' And then I might ask, How do you think they felt when they heard that?'*

7.9   Staff also suggested that shuttle mediation could provide an important preparatory stage for face-to-face. It familiarised the mediator with the issues involved; allows the parties to discuss possible outcomes in advance; facilitates catharsis; allows positive comments made by the party to be emphasised and allows the parties to make best use of the time available to look towards options for the future rather than having to relive the conflict once again in public. Shuttling also adds predictability to a subsequent face-to-face meeting and allows the mediator to structure the way they manage the face-to-face session.

7.10   Secondly, staff spoke positively about the fact that shuttle mediation allowed them to help with more cases than might otherwise be possible and argued that this was better than rejecting cases because one party wanted to engage in face-to-face negotiations. Thirdly, mediators felt that some cases were unsuitable for face-to-face mediation because the dispute was highly charged emotionally. In some cases this was because the parties had been violent towards each other. One mediator explained that they felt a responsibility to the disputants to protect them from unnecessary abuse:

> *If you offer [face-to-face] mediation too soon you can build up*
> *expectations about it being the next step. But there are cases I wouldn't*
> *even think about bringing into face-to-face. Sometimes its just too*
> *volatile. You get someone saying they will staple the other person's lips*
> *together next time they see them and you have to think, 'Hang on, let's*
> *see how this one progresses before we offer face-to-face.'*

7.11 Mediators also expressed concerns about the impact of such behaviour on them: 'There can be such a thing as too much conflict. Face-to-face mediations can be an ordeal. We see tensions, tears, abuse and violence. It's not something that is helpful at the end of the day.'

7.12 Despite these arguments in favour of shuttle mediation, mediators also recognised its limitations and one mediator at the Centre expressed an overall preference for face-to-face meetings between the parties. In reviewing their concerns about shuttle mediation, mediators were influenced by the fact that it could take some time to reach a solution. The co-ordinator gave one example of shuttling between two parties for eight hours in one day. There was also concern that the shuttle method only allowed the mediator to convey views between the parties and did not encourage the public display of emotion or regret to the other side. As one mediator put it to a disputant:

> *We can shuttle between you and go from house to house. The other*
> *option is face-to-face where we can have an open discussion which*
> *I feel personally is the better way. In shuttle I am only the messenger,*
> *I cannot relay your feelings. In a face-to-face you can express how you*
> *feel at the time. We usually come to a written agreement that way.*

What happens on home visits?

7.13 Visits involved a number of process stages which broadly follow in sequence (see figure 7.1). These were: the preliminary stage, the exploratory stage and the issue-seeking stage.

Figure 7.1 Process stages of home visits

Structure of meeting	Skills and techniques

Preliminaries and icebreaking

Focus on dispute

Exploration of issues

Clarification and identification of issues

Seeking options for the future

Identify next steps

Cooling out and exit

✔ Listening

✔ Facilitating catharsis

✔ Assimilating

✔ Translation of negative to positive

✔ Narrowing and expanding issues

✔ Contextualising and managing expectations

✔ De-personalising

a. Preliminaries

7.14   This first stage of the meeting focused on three stages. Firstly, the mediators would introduce themselves to the disputant and verify their identity. Secondly, mediators used 'icebreaking' techniques to put the disputants(s) at their ease. Examples drawn from participant observation include reference to the homely smell of cooking, décor of the residence and photographs of children on the walls. Mediators always waited to be directed to a room and asked to sit down.

7.15   The final stage of the preliminaries was a description of the mediator's role and the process. This commonly included a reference to: their independence from the council and brokering role; their experience as neighbour dispute specialists; the confidentiality of the meeting; and a statement to the effect that agreements reached were not legally binding and the mediators had no formal powers to impose solutions on the parties.

b. Exploration of issues

7.16   During this stage the disputant was invited to tell the mediator about the problems they had experienced with their neighbour. The amount of information requested by mediators often depended on the level of contact prior to the visit. In many cases disputants' accounts were naturally forthcoming. However, they were also prompted, or issues clarified, by the mediators posing a series of questions such as:

- Who is involved in the dispute?

- How did the dispute begin?

- What is the history of the relationship and residency?

- How did parties had reacted to what had happened?

- Whether the disputants had taken any action as a result of the dispute?

7.17   Participant observations of visits revealed that this stage of the process could take up a considerable amount of time. Mediators contended that their main aim at this stage of the process was to get an account of the disputant's grievance without appearing partisan or judgmental. The following extract from a participant observation record demonstrates attempts to achieve such a position.

> CLIENT: *They weren't here when I moved in. When they did move in they used to do DIY until 11.30 at night. I used to do a morning job so I went up there. It didn't stop until 1.30 in the morning so I made several complaints. The housing office told me I wasn't the only one.*
>
> MEDIATOR: *They told you that?*
>
> CLIENT: *Yes, and I know the lady before me had problems. The kids up there get up at 6.30am. They don't need to make so much noise.*
>
> MEDIATOR: *So, let's get the issues clear. It was DIY in the early hours.*
>
> CLIENT: *Yeah, it went on for a long time. I think they got angry about me complaining. Then I got angry and retaliated. Then I stopped because it wasn't doing any good.*
>
> MEDIATOR: *I can understand that.*

7.18   It can be seen that throughout this encounter the mediator does not express an opinion about the validity of the complaint. Instead, they prompt the further unravelling of the disputant's account by reference to what they have already been told.

c. Seeking options for the future

7.19   Once the complainant's or respondent's grievance has been explored, mediators commonly moved on to a stage in which they tried to identify resolution options. This stage of the process usually opened with the disputant being asked what they want to achieve and how they thought mediation could help them to achieve that outcome. In interviews, all the mediators stressed how important it was to encourage the parties to come up with their own options. Proponents of mediation commonly suggest that one of the benefits of mediation is that settlement is more likely to work because resolution options are owned by the parties. The practice also reflects respect for party autonomy and empowerment. Mediators phrased their prompts in a number of ways, such as, 'So, how is it going to go on?', 'You can't carry on like this, so how can things progress?', 'Any ideas what we can do?', 'Where do we go from here?' and 'If we said to you, "What do you want tomorrow?", what would it be?'.

7.20   Where such prompts did not result in identifying solutions, mediators at SMC were prepared to make their own suggestions. Mediators often gave advice about practical resolution options. Advice given in this context included:

- telling neighbours when rubbish was being put out for collection;

- the use of herbal pellets to stop cats defecating on the lawn;

- using a chopping block rather than the floor to cut objects on;

- putting rubber feet on chairs;

- securing a towel over the top of a door to stop it banging;

- wearing slippers in the home.

For some proponents and critics of mediation, such prompts constitute unjustified intervention in dispute resolution, but such practices have been justified as a way of avoiding impasse. In making these suggestions, SMC mediators also drew on their experience of practical and simple solutions which could diffuse the dispute.

7.21   Towards the close of the visit, the mediators would re-cap on the issues which had been identified, the things that the disputant would like to achieve and the possible options for change. They would also commonly confirm whether there were comments or opinions they would like the mediator to convey to the other disputant. As the visit came to a close, there was always a 'cooling out' period in which there was some social 'chit-chat' to bring the session to a close. The techniques used were very similar to the icebreakers used at the beginning of the visit. Following on from the visit with the complainant, the mediators would attempt to meet with the respondent using the same process stages and resolution techniques. If necessary, further shuttling could occur between the parties' homes. The purposes of the shuttling process were to identify common ground, explore the full range of issues in dispute, take messages from one party to the other and share suggestions about how the problems experienced might be resolved or minimised.

Face-to-face mediation

7.22 A small number of cases also progress further, to face-to-face mediation. We have argued above that although most commentators place emphasis on this kind of mediation, our research suggests that it is the exception rather than the norm. Of the 168 SMC case files analysed for this study, just 20 (12 per cent) resulted in a face-to-face mediation taking place. In part this can be accounted for by the reluctance of the parties to engage in this form of resolution. But, it was also clear from interviews and participant observations that mediators filtered out those case they did not think would be suitable for mediation. This approach was justified by reference to the contention that they were in charge of process and the parties were in charge of content. In reality, this meant that face-to-face mediation was not discussed with disputants as a possibility. As one mediator explained:

> *We will mention it but we sort of 'pooh-pooh' it a little bit. We wait and see what we think would be most suitable because using face-to-face with the wrong case could just run the chance of reviving the dispute.*

7.23 Because of the relatively low number of face-to-face mediations, the research team placed emphasis on observing and understanding the process of shuttle mediation. However, the research manager was able to observe a handful (five) of face-to-face mediations and a number of other case were also discussed with mediators in interview.

7.24 Mediators also commented on the ways in which meeting face to face changed the dynamics of the dispute. As one mediator contended, 'We can relay feelings but we can't relay emotions.' Other mediators also argued that in some cases it was important for the parties to witness and understand the strength of feeling which the dispute aroused. This was particularly the case where the mediators felt that resolution would be enhanced by a personal apology. One mediator explained: 'In some cases face-to-face can actually inflame the dispute. But if you choose the right case you can find that an apology made in person can be extremely powerful.'

7.25 Face-to-face mediations commonly occurred at SMC premises. They were conducted in a basement room located in between the kitchen and staff offices. A window has recently been added to the room to give it more natural light and since the evaluation began the premises including the mediation room have undergone substantial refurbishment in order to make it more comfortable for the parties. The mediation room is furnished with low easy chairs around a circular table (figure 7.2). In exceptional cases a face-to-face mediation might be held off-site. Examples of this given in interviews included: mediations conducted at a volunteer's home where this was in close proximity to the disputants; the former offices of SMC since wheelchair access was a problem at their premises; and a housing office when one of the parties had problems arranging transport.[2]

Figure 7.2 Arrangement of the parties at a face-to face mediation session

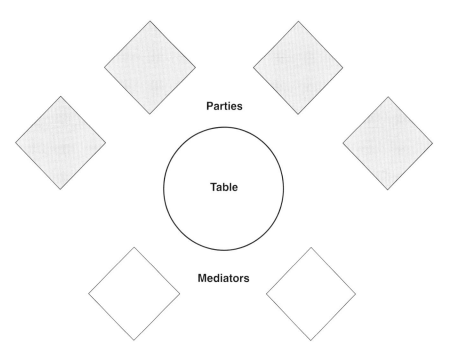

7.26 When the parties arrive they are shown into separate rooms until the mediation commences and offered refreshments. Face-to-face meetings are commonly co-mediated by two mediators[3] and the lead mediator is invariably the same person who has conducted the visit. The principal parties to the dispute are usually accompanied by a partner or friend. The parties are asked not to bring children as SMC do not feel that they have the facilities to accommodate them. However, disputants have on occasion been unable to make babysitting arrangements and in these situations members of the Centre have offered to babysit for them. The exception to this rule is where the dispute actually involves the children, a possibility that SMC were coming to recognise as more and more significant in intergenerational and neighbour disputes. In these circumstances, children in conflict might have their aspect of the larger dispute mediated off-site and separately from the disputing parents.

7.27   Seating arrangements in mediation are often considered significant. some mediators are concerned that the parties do not literally sit face-to-face as this encourages them to see each other as adversaries. In line with this, SMC mediators have adopted a triangular configuration of chairs in which disputants face the mediator rather than each other. It was argued that this encourages the parties to address their comments through the mediator (see figure 7.2.).

Control of process

7.28   Mediation practitioners who adhere to the popular model of mediation frequently make a distinction between; interventionist techniques used to control the process of mediation which they consider legitimate and interventionist techniques used to control outcome which are considered illegitimate (Roberts 1993). Academic critics of the process of mediation have argued that a control of process can effect the outcome achieved by limiting or prioritising the issues in discussion (Mulcahy *et al.* 2000; Dingwall and Greatbatch 1993). Participant observations of face-to-face mediations provided useful case studies of active control of the mediation process. The mediators laid stress on the importance of 'giving accounts rather than taking accounts' in face-to-face mediation. By this they meant that it was the mediators rather than the parties who summarised the issues in dispute at the opening of each face-to-face session. Mediators drew on the description of grievances given to them on visits to the parties' homes which occurred prior to face-to-face contact. The practice provided an opportunity for mediators to translate issues and they mentioned that they used it as an opportunity to prioritise the issues in dispute and make more effective use of the time available. In their presentation, they would usually start with the more trivial issues and build up to those which were most important to the parties. After each account was given the parties were given an opportunity to assess the accuracy of what had been said and to add additional issues to those being considered if necessary.

7.29   This approach was justified by mediators on a number of grounds. They claimed that it allowed them to focus the parties on a set number of issues which the mediators had been given an opportunity to reflect on in advance. They were keen to avoid 'flashpoints' or unpredictable outbursts or raising of new issues in the middle of the mediation. Mediators felt that by setting the agenda at the beginning of the mediation they were pinpointing the issues to be discussed. It was also argued that the process added to mediator credibility. SMC staff were concerned that they would lose the confidence of disputants if they asked them to repeat what they had spent some time discussing during visits. One mediator put it thus;

> *In face-to-face we don't take accounts we give accounts. If we asked them for their account they would think, 'Why? I've already told you.' They want us to do it. We ask them to add to it if they want to. We re-phrase what they say, we don't change it.*

Allowing mediators to recap on issues was also seen to provide an opportunity for mediators to focus on the future rather than dwell on the past. As the co-ordinator explained: 'The only way to get some people in to face-to-face is not to talk about the past. It's not a case of a trickle of water under the bridge, it's a whole torrent.'

7.30 Each of these justifications suggests that, contrary to their visions of how mediation should occur in practice, mediators may encourage discussion in a certain direction. An inevitable impact of this may be to prioritise the discussion of certain resolution options. It may also effect the tendencies of the parties to compromise as some issues may be of greater importance to one disputant than another. The findings suggest that the practice of mediation is not always as flexible as proponents would have us think. Moreover, it supports the contention that control over process and outcome is exercised in overt but also covert and subtle ways by mediators (see, also, Grillo 1991; Dingwall and Greatbatch 1993). We return to these themes in the next chapter.

Techniques used during shuttle and face-to-face mediation

7.31 During the course of each of the stages outlined above, mediators relied on a number of techniques to bring disputes to resolution. In this section, the major techniques employed are reviewed. These are facilitating communication, translation of issues, the use of empathy and the control of process.

Facilitating communication

7.32 Mediators were keen to stress that a core component of mediation was its ability to open up and improve channels of communication between the parties. The process was seen as educative in that it allows the parties to be exposed to someone else's point of view and challenged by it. In time, mediators hoped that this would allow an understanding and possible sympathy for points of view other than their own. In this way, the parties were encouraged to reflect on the validity of their own position and that of the other disputant. As one mediator explained: 'Saying they [the other disputant] don't normally listen is not adequate. In a number of cases the parties have never sat within one and a half feet of each other.'

Box 7.2: Information flow

'Having a new carpet will make a difference. She needs to know that you are going to do that soon.'

'Can I tell them you are not well?'

'Is there anything you don't want me to mention apart from the fraud. Perhaps the kids being left unattended. I wonder if that is useful'

'I will mention to him all the positive things you have said today. About the parcels and the fact that you are having the insulation done.'

7.33 Research on mediation has stressed the importance of maintaining a constant flow of information between the parties and this has been identified as a way of constantly moving the dispute forward and avoiding impasse. A common technique used in pursuit of this goal was asking the parties whether certain information given in confidential shuttle meetings could be conveyed to the other side. Examples of the use of this technique appear in box 7.2. It can be seen that these also include the giving of advice about information which might be detrimental to dispute settlement. The quotations also suggest ways in which mediators can filter or encourage the exchange of certain information.

7.34 In many of the examples given the mediator is seeking permission to relay specific pieces of information to the other party. Mediators also encouraged an information flow by retaining a discretion to pass on all the information gleaned in the private meeting unless the disputant specified pieces of information that they did not want to be conveyed. In other situations mediators were more proactive in encouraging the parties to reflect on the necessity for movement to be made through the provision of information to the other side. Thus, in one case a mediator suggested: 'Is there anything other than you telling her to fuck off that I could mention?'

7.35 Mediators might also encourage the transmission of information about the impression created in shuttling. Most commonly this involved a request to convey that the complaint about a neighbour was not personal or that compliments had also been made about them such as their child-rearing skills or a feeling of gratitude for an abatement of noise. Mediators were keen in interviews with the research team to make clear the importance of accentuating the positive in moving towards resolution. As one mediator suggested to a disputant: 'Things can be changed easily if people want them. That is why I need to tell her the good things first.'

The use of empathy

7.36 It was apparent from participant observations that mediators make extensive use of empathy to resolve disputes between neighbours. Mediators contended that empathy is used for two different reasons. Firstly, it allows mediators to demonstrate that they are capable of understanding the problems faced by tenants. Viewed in this way, the technique allows them to stress the importance of an ideology which underpins community mediation; that mediators are from the community they seek to serve and understand the problems faced by residents. In the first category, mediators commonly referred to having experienced similar problems with neighbours or having reacted in the same way as the disputant in response to a complaint. Secondly, it was argued that use of empathy was a way to validate the client's experience without passing judgement and that it underpins the empowerment of the client.

7.37 In almost a third of observed visits, mediators sought to validate disputants' sense of grievance by indicating that their reaction was to be expected and normal by referring to shared standards. Comments in the former category included: 'It's human nature to justify yourself, that's natural behaviour.'; 'When she comes to the door, she's wound you up and you become defensive, that is very normal.'; 'When you are in conflict, you find this sort of behaviour.' As the last quotation suggests, such observations often strove to construct disputes as unusual; as outlandish events which encouraged people to act out of character. It has been argued that by using such techniques, mediation operates as a form of confession in which the mediator hears transgressions from acceptable behaviour and forgives them (Pavlich *et al.*, 1996).

7.38 In the same vein, it was regularly asserted that disputes were capable of transforming people's personalities and that this was to be expected. The following comment by a mediator was typical of this category:

> *When you go up there, even when you think you are being polite, you aren't. You are fuming and all the emotions come out in your body language. Confrontation is not the best form of communication to use. The best way to explain it is that it all builds up and when you go up there you are not just going up there about one thing. It is all the things that have been happening for ages. They build up.*

Mediators regularly made reference to shared values, often involving allusions to disappearing standards and idealised visions of past communities. Comments in this group included: 'Times have completely changed, but we have to live with it.'; and, 'Society has changed, You used to be able to leave your key with your neighbours, not anymore.'

7.39   Interviews with mediators also suggested that they were wary of empathising with the parties too much. They displayed a tension between the perceived need to aspire to neutrality and their standing as a fellow member of the community. As one mediator explained:

> *You have to be really careful because agreeing with something they say can get you into trouble later on. You might be in someone's flat and they are complaining about their neighbour's garden and they ask you to look at it. You might say, 'Oh, yes. It is bad.' and then, if they come face-to-face, that person could say in public, 'Well, you saw that garden and you agreed with it.' And, well, that's it. You really lose your neutrality then.*

7.40   Such wariness also extended beyond the words used to facial expressions and mannerisms. One mediator explained how she had been alerted in training to the fact that her facial expressions were too explicit and suggestive of sympathy for the disputants' plight. As the same mediator put it: 'You have to make sure those thoughts go through your head, not your face or your mouth.'

Conclusion

7.41   This chapter has highlighted the ways in which SMC staff mediate disputes. Although the mediation process is considered to be flexible, disputes which are pursued beyond referral tend to be managed according to a similar pattern. Unlike many other settings in which mediation occurs, community mediation at SMC is best viewed as a process rather than a discrete event. Disputants are commonly contacted by phone to discuss their grievance, and visited in their home. Occasionally, they meet face to face. Data collected for this study demonstrate that some disputants do not want to meet face to face but that the paucity of face-to-face mediation can more accurately be accounted for by mediator preferences. SMC mediators argued that shuttle mediating between the parties' homes gave them much more control over the processing of the dispute and allowed them to contain what might otherwise become extremely volatile interactions.

7.42   Mediators use a considerable number of techniques in their attempts to bring the dispute to resolution. Shuttle mediation affords them considerable control over the type of communication channelled between the parties and mediators use these possibilities to neutralise and de-personalise the grievance. The ways in which they translate issues also reflect an ideological commitment to conciliatory approaches to conflict resolution and this is suggested by their frequent reference to shared norms and the dangers of pursuing grievances in adversarial settings, such as the courts. The roles discussed are those anticipated by mediation gurus. In the chapter which follows, we pursue many of these themes and consider the variety of roles, other than mediator which are performed by SMC staff in practice.

Endnotes

1. It was not possible to observe telephone calls with the parties in any formal way as they could occur at any time of the day and structured observation would have required a constant surveillance of mediators. However, the project manager spent so much time on site at SMC analysing the files and attending visits that a large number of telephone conversations were witnessed. Moreover, the issue of telephone contact was raised with each of the mediators in interview.

2   Mediators also cited one instance in which a face-to-face mediation had occurred in one of the parties' homes. This was considered to be an exceptional case as it was considered crucial that each party felt equally at ease at the selected location.

3. This was the principal reason why it was not possible for the research team to observe more face-to-face mediations. There was some concern that the addition of another person would make the room seem over-crowded.

Chapter 8: The many roles of mediators

Introduction

8.1 In the last chapter, we presented an account of mediation which outlined the various ways in which mediators attempt to comply with an ideal model in which they are neutral and facilitative. The data presented revealed that mediators attempt to avoid a partisan or evaluative stance in dealing with disputes. However, it was also suggested that this ideal can be difficult to achieve and that mediators frame the content and process of discussion in subtle ways which may have an impact on outcome. In this chapter, we consider the extent to which the ideal model aspired to is ever completely attainable. We examine the various ways in which Southwark Mediation Centre (SMC) mediators challenge the feasibility and appropriateness of prescribed boundaries in the course of attempting to resolve disputes. The chapter then goes on to consider the ways in which the data presented challenge the possibility of neutrality and facilitation being achieved.

A flexible approach to process and neutrality

8.2 Mediators at SMC favoured a flexible approach to dispute resolution. This is not unusual amongst mediators, but it is usually argued that flexibility should be limited to process and setting. Recent changes in the way that work is organised at the Centre and a change of co-ordinator have facilitated a more experimental approach to dispute handling at SMC, a change which was universally welcomed by staff. As one of the mediators explained:

> We are open to all techniques. Staff are encouraged to reflect on current practices and think of new ways forward with every dispute. In many ways that approach has allowed the centre and the mediators within it to grow. We have grown because we have been given the opportunity to.

8.3 The approach is all the more interesting because their deliberations about process have been divorced from national debates about the development of community mediation. In the years prior to the research taking place, mediators at the Centre had not attended national conferences or read widely on the subject of mediation. As a result, the style of mediation to which they now adhere has developed in something of a vacuum and with reference to local needs.

8.4   The 'modes' of mediation adopted by SMC mediators reflect a pragmatic attitude to disputes and some dissatisfaction with the more prescriptive model of mediation practice prescribed by some practitioners. In the words of the co-ordinator, 'We will do whatever it takes to help the parties and resolve the conflict.' This may involve flexibility in where, when and how they manage disputes and involve talking to the parties on the phone, visiting them in their homes, suggesting that they attend for a face-to-face session and asking them to attend a follow-up session. But it also involved flexibility in the ways in which the mediation was conducted. Staff at SMC expressed frustration at the more inflexible approaches to community mediation which were encouraged by other practitioners within the mediation community and the emphasis on a formulaic face-to-face model. One of the mediators described how she had been asked at a national conference to talk trainees through a video of the mediation process produced by Mediation UK. Having watched the video, she felt unable to undertake the training because the mediatory style suggested was so out of line with the approach adopted at Southwark. In her words:

> *I told them that I was sorry but there was no way I could stand up there and teach with that video as though that were the 'right' way to do it. But, if they would let me, I would stand up there with it and tell the group that there were a lot of examples of how not to do it. To tell you the truth I think our model is much more advanced because it allows you to take reality into account. We are flexible. What happens with one client will not work with another.*

8.5   A review of other research on mediation suggests that such evaluations of the differences between SMC and other mediation agencies may be slightly exaggerated since most agencies would lay claim to flexibility. But, what remains interesting about developments at SMC is their attempts to grapple with the impossibilities of dominant facilitative models of mediation. One example of this was the way in which mediators talked about the necessity of stepping out of role and into what one called 'their everyday personality' in the course of mediations. The image conveys the dominance of the idea of the mediator as an empty emotional vessel and the reality of their ability to achieve such neutrality or remoteness. Stepping out of role occurred when mediators found themselves angered or frustrated by an encounter with a disputant. They submitted that at times it was difficult to maintain impartiality. They were concerned that much of the training which was available for mediators assumed that they could keep negative evaluations of disputants at bay and that this did not reflect the reality. As the co-ordinator explained:

> *It's just not real to expect people to do this job and not form views. We are like everyone else … just human. My worry is that in training you are often told that you are not trained to have thoughts. It sounded great and then you get out there and you have them and it makes you feel as if you are doing something wrong. It really used to destroy me. We have to accept that these things happen and find ways of dealing with it. Our mediators actually feel liberated by that common-sense approach.*

8.6   The approach adopted at SMC was for mediators to be encouraged to identify negative or biased reactions to disputants which fell outside what was 'acceptable' behaviour, voice them if necessary to a colleague and then try to put them aside as 'passing thoughts'. Their approach reflected the fact that mediation can be emotionally intensive and that, as key players in the process, mediators were also likely to have to deal with the emotional aftermath of sessions. It also encouraged mediators to reflect on the core values which should govern their behaviour and the ways in which they were constantly challenged.

8.7   But Southwark mediators 'stepped out of role' in other ways which challenged the boundaries of acceptable practice as prescribed in many texts on the subject. They performed a number of roles in the course of dealing with disputes, some of which overlapped with the functions of mediators and others which remained distinct from traditional formulations of the role. Much of the discussion of roles contained in this chapter serves to question the assumption that mediators can come to a dispute value-free and that their normative frameworks have no impact on the way they manage disputes. Socio-legal scholars have placed emphasis on the importance of understanding the inevitability of flexibility in the performance of third-party dispute resolution tasks. In his work on the judiciary, Galanter (1981) has drawn attention to the various roles they adopt including, most notably, the use of mediatory techniques to achieve out-of-court settlement. These roles did not form part of the formal or traditional model of adjudication to which the system they operated within ascribed. Rather, they reflected a pragmatic and informal approach to achieving what they considered to be their goal. Similarly, in their comprehensive review of research on third-party roles, Black and Baumgartner (1983) argue that the 10 major support and settlement roles they identify are far from discrete. Rather, they suggest that third parties in disputes alter both the nature of their intervention and their level of partisanship depending on the needs of the disputants and other circumstances. Using this model in a hospital setting, Lloyd-Bostock and Mulcahy (1994) have contended that managers attempting to resolve disputes between patients and doctors adopt a chameleon-style approach to dispute resolution which changes with the circumstances of the case, the issues and personalities of those involved.

Mediation ambassador

8.8   However neutral mediators may claim to be in their handling of disputes, they are advocates of SMC and mediation. Statements made by mediators in the course of shuttle mediations observed by the research team provide examples of such partisanship. Many of these statements served to establish the credibility of the mediator as a third party in the dispute and reflected a 'sales pitch'. The mediators remained committed to the resolution of disputes through conciliatory means. Comments about the success of SMC and the superiority of mediation over other forms of resolution were not uncommon and were founded in positive evaluations of the success of mediation and negative evaluations of the alternatives. Mediators also referred to their high success rate;[1] the fact that staff at the centre had 12 years' experience of dealing with complaints; and their view that mediation was a commonsensical approach to dispute settlement. Some of their comments are reproduced in box 8.1. These reflect a mixture of persuasive techniques involving the exhortation of the benefits of mediation as a pragmatic and more peaceful resolution of disputes as well as a vision of the alternative of going to court as hostile. Mediators often made reference to the problems of legal proceedings in terms of the evidential burden required of the parties, for instance, that domestic noise was difficult to prove, and the difficulties of enforcing injunctions. One mediator described the value of face-to-face mediation over litigation in the following way:

> *It is about two people coming closer to the fence, meeting at the fence and thinking about what has happened. When the law gets involved you end up in opposite corners. You need to understand each other's point of view but it needs to be done in a controlled setting, [face-to-face] offers this.*

> **Box 8.1: The superiority of mediation to law**
>
> 'Well, you said that you don't want to meet face-to-face. We can shuttle it. You have chosen a very amicable route to settle your dispute.'
>
> 'Your housing officer is good. She puts mediation at the top of the list. It is a very good way to resolve disputes.'
>
> 'I don't know any other way to bring the stress peaks down except through mediation ... the law won't do anything ... [mediation] is about two people coming closer to the fence, meeting at the fence and thinking about what has happened. When the law gets involved you end up in opposite corners.'
>
> 'If you took them to court they would get legal advice and it would all be pulled apart. I am just warning you that it could easily get thrown out of court. It comes down to you to prove it in court.'

8.9   At times mediation was also favourably compared to council handling of complaints and disputes. As one mediator explained to a disputant: 'The housing office ends up with two people in dispute that they don't know what to do with. We get it then.'; and again, 'What happens in Southwark is that you complain to [the housing officer] then she counter-complains to him and then he end ups with two neighbours complaining to him and he does not know what to do and then we get it.'; 'I would say that they probably have the same problems with the housing officer as you do. But housing do nothing.'

8.10 Since Southwark residents appear to know relatively little about mediation, these attempts at describing the process reflect a need to do this by reference to other more familiar dispute resolution mechanisms. But, the presentation of the positive aspects of mediation and negative aspects of the alternatives suggests that it is a sales pitch, rather than a discussion of alternative ways of handling the dispute which is at stake. Greatbatch and Dingwall (1989) have sought to explain such attempts at establishing mediation as a superior form of dispute resolution as part of a broader push to establish a market share for mediation services. This desire to heighten the profile of mediation is also reflected at national level in the move towards accreditation of services and the increase in educational programmes. Despite such efforts, mediation remains relatively unpopular with litigants where entry to the programme remains voluntary.

Translator

8.11 Another way in which mediators moved the negotiations towards settlement was by facilitating the translation of issues. By claiming autonomy over process rather than content, proponents of mediation commonly maintain that the definition of the issues in dispute is the remit of the disputants. By way of contrast, academic commentaries on disputes have stressed the inevitability of all third parties taking part in the translation of allegation. In their review of the anthropological literature on disputes, Mather and Yngvesson (1980-1) stress the importance of third parties in refining the issues at stake. They have argued that the transformation of a dispute can involve antagonists and third parties in three processes. Firstly, there is 'rephrasing', that is, a reformulation of the issues in dispute into a public discourse. After rephrasing the new account of the dispute will continue to reflect the perspectives of the antagonists, but it is suggested that this will also reflect the interests of any third parties. Secondly, expansion involves a challenging of existing established categories for defining the ambit of the dispute. In this way accepted frameworks are 'stretched'. Thirdly, there is 'narrowing', a process through which established categories for classifying events and relationships are imposed in a way which make it amenable to conventional management procedures. They argue that narrowing is particularly common amongst officials in formalised grievance procedures where there are routine-driven ways of handling claims. Established categories in this sense are those which are linked to the interests of the third party managing the dispute.

8.12 The transcripts of participant observations provided examples of a number of ways in which disputants' grievances were translated in subtle ways, many of which fall into the categories identified by Mather and Yngvesson (1980-1). Frequently, mediators 'externalised' the cause of the dispute by laying the cause of conflict outside the parties. Most commonly, this took the form of attributing the cause of noise to poor insulation or architectural design rather than to the parties themselves. The following comments were typical of this category: 'Well, you have some common ground. Insulation, that is the problem between all of you. This property is 100 years old.' 'When these properties were built, they were built for radiograms, not stereos and amplified music.' And, 'Well, part of the problem is that your living room is above a bedroom. They don't do that anymore. So that when you are living, she is trying to sleep.' In one sense, these translations 'narrowed' the issues in dispute by imposing an established category on the grievants' accounts. All the mediators interviewed were clear that, in their view, poor insulation caused a high proportion of disputes. They also had the effect of neutralising the grievance and identifying common ground for the parties. If the problem of poor insulation is blamed on the council, such translation could also have the effect of 'rephrasing' the grievance to a collective problem. An example of comment in this category was: 'Ninety per cent of the cases that we have are due to poor insulation. You would think that someone in Southwark Council would take note.' However, it was much more common for such translation to neutralise the dispute by suggesting that poor insulation was just something that residents had to live with.

8.13 There were other examples of attempts at neutralisation of the grievance, through narrowing disputes. Mediators explained how they made a conscious effort to de-personalise the dispute by making a distinction between the issues and the people involved. As one mediator explained to a disputant:

> *People can see problems as personal attacks, as a claim that they are in the wrong ... We need to re-establish that you are not complaining because you don't like them but because you feel it is unfair.*

And again:

> *The main reason I have come to see you is that one of your neighbours has some concerns about noise. It is not a problem with your children, but with the noise.*

8.14 Mediators also challenged the ways in which blame was being attributed by encouraging the parties to reflect on whether the nuisance was malicious or intentional. The following examples are typical: 'Maybe the people upstairs are not aware of the problems they are causing.' and 'Sometimes people work shift-work and forget that others aren't working the same patterns.' In some cases, mediators were more directive:

> *In defence of people that live in upstairs flats, she probably isn't aware of the noise she is making ... I don't think people realise the noise you hear, they need to understand. (PO18)*

And again:

> *If you put a camera in both flats you may find that it wasn't anything they were aware of. I am not saying that they don't do things deliberately, people sometimes do. But they have got used to living in a certain way. (PO3)*

Peacemaker

8.15   The adoption of a facilitative stance does not necessarily bring with it an assumption that there will be a peaceful resolution to the dispute. Moreover, critics of informalism have expressed concern that the suppression of conflict may also be used to suppress open discussion and the concerns of the disadvantaged. Viewed in this way, conflict and argument can be seen as having a positive value as a way of bringing to light injustices and new perspectives. Proponents of mediation suggest that an important function of mediators, and possible end point of the mediation, is to clarify the issues at stake. This is particularly the case in the transformative model of mediation which is much less settlement orientated than others and increasingly influential in the field of community mediation. Even within a settlement orientated model, mediation may, in reality, function best within an adversarial setting. Meschievitz's (1991) work on a medical negligence mediation pilot scheme in the United States concluded that, although a high proportion of cases mediated subsequently went on to be adjudicated in the courts, the mediation process had served to narrow the issues in dispute and served the function of an early neutral evaluation of the strengths and weaknesses of the parties respective cases. Does a commitment to a facilitative role in which neutrality is preserved deny the possibility of mediators framing disputes within a normative framework which values peace?

8.16   Formal settlement of disputes can clearly be achieved without an abeyance of the parties' animosity towards each other. This is most obvious in studies of the courts which have demonstrated that the parties often continue to feel a sense of grievance and dissatisfaction after judgement has been reached or formal settlement achieved (Mulcahy *et al.* 2000). However, an important contention of many mediators is that mediation serves to resolve grievances as well as working towards settlement. In this way it is claimed that mediation can achieve more lasting resolutions. Thus, mediation serves to fulfil the much more difficult task of *transforming* the way the disputants look at their grievance so that the positions of the parties are changed in a way which makes resolution much more possible.

Box 8.2: Accentuating the positive

'It is very positive that you feel that you may need each other some time in the future. It is good to think of the future.'

'When you mentioned that you thought someone was being murdered, you must have been very worried about her.'

'Things can be changed easily if people want them to. That is why we need to tell her the good things first.'

'If you have been putting up with this noise for eight years then you are very tolerant.'

I will let them know you want this sorted out … My job is to calm the situation not fuel it. You want it sorted out. Nobody likes disputes. They probably feel the same. It adds stress to everyday life.'

'You want peace and quiet and you might find that they want the same.'

8.17   Despite the possibilities of peaceful settlement being abandoned as an appropriate end point in all mediated cases, researchers have drawn attention to the tendencies for mediators to work towards this goal. In their study of a community-based mediation programme situated in a social services agency, Silbey and Merry (1986) drew attention to the ways in which one group of mediators based their activity on the assumption that misunderstandings and failures of communication, rather than fundamental differences of opinion, are the source of conflict and that encouraging the sharing of information about the parties' positions and feelings should lead to consensus and harmony.

8.18   Mediators at SMC commonly encouraged a peaceful resolution to the dispute and its settlement. They did this by accentuating the ways in which the parties agreed as well as their disagreement and by stressing the positive rather than the negative aspects of the dispute. They frequently asserted that their aim was to establish a conciliatory framework within which disputing parties could interact in future. As the co-ordinator explained:

> *It's about the future. It's not about forgive and forget. It's about letting go, about opening up a new chapter. It's also about discussing the repercussions of not letting go. What it comes down to is being really honest with people.*

8.19 It has already been suggested that mediators thought it was patronising to expect the parties to become good friends as a result of the process. They felt that, if they made suggestions, it would seriously undermine their credibility as community mediators. However, they did work hard to stress the positive aspects of the disputants' relationship and encouraged the parties to see the other disputant in as positive a light as possible. They did this in three different ways: by accentuating common ground between the parties; by encouraging a positive approach to the issues raised; and by encouraging them to communicate positive feelings. Each of these served to encourage a peaceful resolution of disputes and conciliatory approach to grievance resolution.

8.20 In a number of instances this involved mediators advising against violence and confrontation with the other party in the dispute. Typical comments included: 'All the people involved are fuelling off each other. You become the big bad monster. The best way to break someone's view of you is to show them you are not like that.'; and 'Perhaps that is something you need, some techniques for calming down, a walk is very good.' In these statements, emphasis is put on the value of maintaining a peaceful equilibrium in the interests of discouraging an exacerbation of grievances.

> **Box 8.3: Conveying the positive**
>
> 'When I spoke to her she said she wants no animosity. She said a lot of positive things about you.'
>
> 'I've been upstairs to see Kylie and Jason and I got a very positive response.'
>
> 'So, you are grateful for the quiet you have had recently. It might be useful for her to know that.'

8.21 Emphasis was also put on the general value of looking at things in a positive light. Conciliatory comments were much more likely to be 'rewarded' with praise from mediators than negative ones (see box 8.2). Mediators also encouraged the parties to let them convey positive comments to the other disputants. Even the sharing of views on what was at issue could be presented in a positive fashion. In one case the mediator opened discussion in a home visit by asserting: 'I have visited your neighbour. I will relay what was said back to you. You have some common ground; children and aggressiveness.' Other examples of this tendency are show in Box 8.4. The ways in which the parties were encouraged to adopt a positive stance were also accentuated by the fact that mediators never rewarded the negative.

Counsellor

8.22   Mediators also spend a significant amount of their time in counselling. Like interactions with disputants, this did not necessarily involve them stepping out of role, as the therapeutic aspects of mediation are commonly emphasised by practitioners. However, it has been argued that encouraging the discussion of emotional aspects of disputes is not necessarily an integral part of mediating. Silbey and Merry (1986) have argued that two distinct models of mediation can be observed; those which encourage bargaining and those which encourage a more therapeutic approach. In the latter model, the parties are encouraged to engage in a full expression of their feelings and attitudes. Mediators in this style describe the purpose of mediation as an effort to help people reach mutual understanding through managing personal relationships rather than the attribution of right and wrong.

8.23   The research conducted for this report demonstrated that neighbour disputes can evoke intense emotions and that a therapeutic approach to problems was favoured by mediators in the study. It was recognised that in addition to the problems caused by the dispute the parties may also be experiencing other problems which can add to their levels of stress. Genn's (1999) recent study of the incidence of disputes suggests that conflicts between neighbours often run in parallel with on-going problems with money. Interviews with mediators and housing officers confirmed that counselling about other problems being experienced by individual disputants was an important aspect of their work. Significantly, housing officers commonly argued that this was something that they did not get sufficient time to do properly and praised mediators for the time and trouble they took to support residents in this way. Many commented that the role was one which had traditionally been adopted by housing officers. Moreover, a handful of disputants interviewed for this study asserted that the mediator they had contact with was the first person who had really taken the trouble to listen to them. Time is clearly an important factor. As one complainant said:

> *We sat down and we had a really good chat. I felt much better after that. She wasn't in a rush, she just sat there and listened and I felt like she really understood what I was talking about. I got it off my chest.*

8.24   In the words of another: 'There wasn't any hurry and she seemed to be prepared to sit there all day and listen if called to.'

8.25   The need for catharsis and to let disputants tell their story was confirmed by the mediators in the study. Displays of emotion were not uncommon in discussions with disputants. In one case the 'counselling' stage of a home visit took 70 minutes and the account of the difficulties experienced by the disputant spanned 29 years of their life. During the course of the discussion, the disputant broke down in tears four times. One mediator explained how essential a part of the process it was in the following terms:

> *Well, you ask them what's been happening that's upset them and it's like, whoosh!. It all comes at you – the neighbours, the council, the relatives – and after about half an hour of listening and probing, you think, right, now is the time to start mediating this.*

8.26　For SMC mediators, the role of counsellor was seen as fairly integral to the mediation process and placed them in Silbey and Merry's (1986) therapeutic mould. Mediators identified a number of skills they had developed in common with counsellors; listening, empathising, clarifying, probing as to why certain events had the effect they did.

Adviser

8.27　In contrast to the notion of the neutral mediator, SMC staff were also prepared to give advice to the disputants about other services in the borough which can help them sort out social problems underlying the dispute, such as mental health and poverty. Of the various roles presented, the role of advice-giver is probably the one most likely to be described by mediators as 'stepping out of role'. Mediators in the study recognised that, in an ideal world, advice giving would not be part of their role as it suggested that a partisan stance was being taken. As we have already suggested, this is often seen as an anathema to any facilitative mediation model. It also requires the mediator to take the lead in the presentation of options, a role which proponents of mediation argue is best left to the parties in dispute. It is frequently argued that the parties are much more likely to abide by an agreement when they have suggested the methods of resolution or abatement themselves.

8.28　A form of advice giving was identified in 17 of the 39 participant observations of visits. Most commonly, the advice given centred on use of state-provided services or the pursuit of a grievance with a state agency. In some cases they suggested that medical advice be sought. In other instances they suggested that disputants contacted the noise team in order to secure firmer evidence of noise nuisance, or that they put pressure on the council to deal with problems underlying the dispute such as rent arrears or the need for the disputant to be re-housed in sheltered accommodation. Examples of the latter include: 'It seems to me you need to move. You need to put pressure on the council and you need to continue the pressure,'; 'I can give you the name of the senior housing officer there. We have all the names back in the office. You have to get through the bureaucracy. Copy all your letters to your MP and make sure you send them registered. Have one spokesperson and channel the complaint.' Mediators also facilitated the handling of underlying social problems by checking with a housing association how a resident could get a higher fence, and by checking up the accuracy of a telephone number. In a small handful of cases mediators suggested that a disputant take legal advice.

8.29 Mediators justified such interventions by reference to the, often dire, social and economic needs of disputants. The advice giving role, though relatively rare, placed mediators most obviously in the positions of advocates for the community of which they were a part. The stress placed on neutrality by mediation gurus appears to deny or, at best, ignore the conflict between the non-partisanship stance expected of mediators and the partisan stance assumed in the selection of mediators from the community in which disputes have arisen. If community mediators are to be valued because of their understanding of local conditions and empathy with disputants, it appears incongruous to talk of neutrality when the dispute involves the State. Community and state may not have to be in opposition to each other – but where they are, what stance can mediators be expected to take? For SMC mediators, the choice was clear.

Message bearer

8.30 In chapter 5 we discussed the concerns that mediators had about the way in which disputes were individualised when many were precipitated by poor housing conditions. One way in which SMC mediators reversed this trend towards complete individualisation of the dispute was to act as message bearers from disputants to the housing office, bringing the concerns of disputants to the attention of state officials. The practice can be characterised as unusual in the sense that it has rarely been discussed in other evaluations of community justice programmes, though often aspired to by critics. Examples of such message-bearing drawn from participant observations include undertakings to mention the problem of a leaking toilet to a housing officer; a broken fence to the estates office and discussing the possibility of a transfer to the responsible housing officer and a social worker. Significantly, it was also clear that the mediators acted as a vehicle through which collective grievances could be channelled to state officials. Individual disputes were dealt with as discrete episodes as far as the parties were concerned, but mediators did keep a mental note of grievances relating to the same issues which they began to frame as *collective* grievances (see box 8.4). A good example of this was provided by disputes about noise which were caused by poorly insulated accommodation. In these cases mediators commonly managed the conflict by attributing blame to the council. They de-personalised the dispute by suggesting to the parties that they were in dispute through no fault of their own. This had the effect of facilitating compromise and raising consciousness about the responsibilities of the state. Moreover, although the details of individual disputes remained confidential, mediators would report collective concerns about poor insulation in blocks of flats and estates. In this way they acted as conduits for the collective voicing and politicisation of dissatisfaction and challenged the priorities and strategies of housing officers through conciliatory informal chats with them.

Box 8.4: Mediating between the individual and state

'The noise team don't [treat tenants as though they are lying about noise levels]. We work with them, they don't. It will be logged on their database.'

'We have no power to get you moved but we can submit a report to the council which might help your case'

'Between you and me we can put pressure on the council.'

'If I think it is impossible I will only let ES know it is inappropriate. I will also contact housing and possibly the senior housing officer and inform them about who is unhappy. At least that will put extra pressure on them'

Box 8.5: Managing expectations

'Then, according to council regulations you are adequately housed.'

'They may feel that you may be using this to get yourself moved. I can tell you that they won't until this dispute is sorted out.'

'Insulation is a problem all over. These are 100-year-old properties.'

When these properties were built, they were built for radiograms not stereos and amplified music.'

8.31 This message-bearing role emphasised the ways in which community mediators are, in practice, both embedded within the community whilst working in partnership with the council. There was also evidence of the possibility of the mediation agency exerting informal pressure on the housing office on behalf of tenants (see box 8.5). It would seem that in addition to mediating between individual disputants SMC staff are mediating between the interests of the state and those of local residents. One mediator made reference to this tendency and justified it in this way:

> *In an ideal world you would not talk to the person who is referring the dispute but, let's be realistic. We deal with the conflict but we need to let the council become aware of what the real problem is. We can deal with the dispute but we can't deal with the problem that is underlying it. That often takes the council or a miracle to change.*

8.32 Mediators also gave examples of how their mediation skills had been brought to bear in performing the role of message bearer for the council. One mediator gave the example of a case involving a terminally ill young man who had been repeatedly playing his music at extremely high volume. Because of a stream of complaints from neighbours the noise team were eventually forced to seize all of his equipment including his daughter's small radio. An SMC mediator was engaged to visit the man and explain to him, in a conciliatory way, why the noise team felt they had been forced into such action.

8.33 It is also clear that an important element of what SMC mediators do is to manage the expectations of disputants. Their work has allowed them to develop an in-depth understanding of the issues that the council has a responsibility to address, the processes used to resolve these problems and the resource limitations of the council. Mediators asserted that if disputes are in the very least exacerbated by living conditions and the stresses of urban life then, while they could deal with a dispute, they could not deal with the environmental or social factors underpinning it. There was a strong sense, in the observations of their work, of them striving towards the accommodation of residents to conditions. Some examples drawn from participant observations are presented in box 8.6.

Conclusion

8.34 Earlier in this report we contended that mediators at SMC felt uncomfortable with mediation training models which did not admit of the possibility of convergence from the ideals of neutrality and facilitation. In this chapter, we have outlined how they have responded to the dilemmas posed by the tension between respecting the ideal and serving the needs of the local community. The issue is one which has been considered by academic researchers, some of whom remain sceptical about the ability of mediators to remain totally neutral or achieve pure facilitation of communication and resolution (see chapter 2). Feminist scholars and legal anthropologists have stressed the impossibility of objectivity and the importance of audiences, even if silent, upon the transformation of issues in dispute. Despite these contentions, the majority of proponents of mediation continue to lay claim to the possibility of the ideal model being achieved.

8.35 Mediators in Southwark have responded to these tensions by adopting a pragmatic approach to the resolution of disputes. They are conscious that until recently they have remained relatively isolated from other mediation organisations and national networks and that their approach may therefore be different. But they have also suggested that it is more advanced and more realistic. It becomes clear that, despite the rhetoric of mediator evangelists, achieving neutrality is a much more difficult task than is often suggested. The issue is one which SMC mediators have become concerned about. What they call their 'advanced' model of mediation is one which recognises that neutrality is a difficult and often impossible goal to achieve. The stance they adopt can also be viewed as an ethical one in which 'stepping out of role' is not seen negatively but as a pragmatic response to the needs of a disadvantaged group.

8.36 What can we learn from the data? The messages are undoubtedly mixed. The ideal of neutrality and facilitation remains important to SMC mediators and they make concerted efforts at achieving it. All the disputants interviewed for this study expressed the view that SMC had not coerced them into any decisions although, interestingly, a number mentioned that they were not worried about neutrality. We have also demonstrated how mediators have valued the peaceful resolution of disputes and the suppression of dissent and anger. But there are times when SMC mediators give advice and relay messages between the state and tenants, most often to raise the concerns of the latter. In this role, they are transformed into political actors with paternalistic concerns for the community within which they work and live. By managing expectations they are often translating demands into what they consider to be more realistic expectations of the state. Unusually, Southwark mediators have shown themselves willing to negotiate with the council on behalf of disadvantaged residents outside a mediation setting. Their attempts to do so allow them to place the process of dispute resolution within a political context and to politicise the disputes. By bearing messages about collective grievances to the housing officers and exerting pressures on them they are challenging the council to fulfil its obligations to tenants. In part, this reflects the fact that the mediators place greater emphasis on their community links and desire to help tenants from their community than the attraction of operating according to what they perceive to be a more formulaic dominant model of mediation practice.

Endnotes

1. In one case mention was made of their 98 per cent success rate with face-to-face mediations.

Chapter 9:   The costs of neighbour disputes

Introduction

9.1   It is frequently asserted that mediation is a cheaper alternative to civil litigation than other forms of dispute resolution. Proponents of informalism do not base their call for greater use of mediation on financial factors. Instead, they prefer to stress the ways in which the process can lead to more constructive settlement of neighbour disputes. But, the debate over the merits of mediation cannot be divorced from considerations of cost. It has also become clear that comparing mediation to litigation in not always a useful exercise when trying to calculate potential savings in costs. The vase majority of disputes between neighbours probably do not even come to the attention of the state, and those that do are handled according to a range of formal and informal methods involving housing officers, the police, social services, NHS workers and many others.

9.2   Concern has been expressed about the costs of neighbour disputes to the state and, in an era in which there are increasing demands on the public sector, the issue of how these costs might be reduced has become the subject of intense debate amongst policy makers, researchers and practitioners. Despite these concerns, there is a paucity of data on the costs of neighbourhood disputes and the issue of whether mediation of these disputes reduces costs remains unaddressed (Dignan *et al.* 1996). Southwark Mediation Centre (SMC) differs from many other community mediation services in that it increasingly employs paid mediators to undertake the administration of the centre and the bulk of the mediations. Mediation is often heralded as a cheaper alternative, but the real costs of community mediation may have been underestimated given that time and resources are often contributed freely by community volunteers. This provided the research team with an almost unique opportunity to evaluate the costs of neighbour mediation when based on a core-funded semi-professional model.

Methods

9.3   Four principles have governed the collection and analysis of data for this study (Knapp 1993). These are that costs should be comprehensively measured, variations identified and explored, like compared with like and cost information integrated with outcomes. However, the collection of such data is not an exact science and the costs of mediation are not easy to compute. In particular, we have become aware that:

- mediation can be introduced to the disputing parties at various points during a dispute. This can make comparison of like with like difficult;

- the costs involved with any dispute can be wide and far-reaching depending on the route that neighbours take and the people or professions that assist or take part in its resolution. Costs accumulate as attempts by various agencies at resolution are made but it can be hard to track involvement. Very often they snowball as no single agency is encouraged to pass over total or sole responsibility to another, without maintaining some form of contact or monitoring. What became clear from the case file analysis and the interviews with housing officers that were conducted for this study was that more than one agency or member of staff would often be working on the same dispute. This was especially true where specialisation was advanced in individual housing offices. Housing officers were often involved in dispute management alongside other departments concerned more specifically with race issues, rent arrears, legal problems and noise as well as external agencies, such as the police and social services. Even when cases were referred to SMC, housing officers continued to have some involvement in case management. Their involvement varied from monitoring progress to carrying out repairs and maintenance that were indicated as contributory to the dispute. These concerns are not new. This observation, that it is difficult to obtain objective information about the costs of introducing mediation, has been echoed by researchers evaluating mediated settlements (Genn 1998; Dignan *et al.* 1996; Conciliation Project Unit 1989).

9.4   Despite these difficulties, evaluating the real costs of mediation was made slightly easier in Southwark. In contrast to other community mediation centres, SMC does not rely heavily on volunteer mediators, administrators, development workers or rent-free premises. Consequently, there are very few hidden subsidies and its accounts reflect the real costs to the Centre of operating and managing disputes between neighbours. In addition, certain limitations have been imposed by the research team on what is was possible for us to achieve within the terms of the original research proposal. The widest definition of costs might incorporate an estimate of the cost of human suffering resulting from neighbour disputes and the knock-on effect for the public sector in terms of hospital visits etc. Undertaking such assessments was a much more ambitious project than was ever anticipated although we have tried to identify a comprehensive list of the types of costs which might arise towards the end of this chapter. For similar reasons we have been unable to compare the costs of mediated cases with those handled in more traditional ways. Data on the latter are extremely hard to come by within the borough, where attempts to collate centralised statistics on dispute management in housing offices have been slow to take effect.

9.5 Instead, we have relied on four sources of data and these are outlined in table 9.1. The table also draws attention to the purpose of each of these datasets and the problems experienced by the research team in accessing them. The costs associated with mediating neighbour disputes are considered independently from any costs that occur before the case is referred to SMC. Instead, the detailed data presented provide an important opportunity to determine the real costs of mediating disputes and the costs of developing, managing and promoting community mediation.

9.6 This chapter is in four sections. In the first section, the sources of funding and costs of running SMC will be examined. Here costs are identified that occur in addition to the management of individual cases. The next section examines the costs to SMC that are associated with the time that mediators spend on various tasks. These are explored through both the specific costs of case management and the costs associated with the time spent on what we have categorised as 'general' SMC tasks such as training and conference attendance. In the third part of the chapter, we use the costs identified in the previous sections to determine the costs of individual cases. Finally, the wider costs that may be associated with neighbour disputes are identified.

Table 9.1 Sources of data, purpose of analysis and problems experienced

Sources of data	Purpose	Problems?
Annual audited reports of SMC	Identification of income, expenditure,overheads and general running costs of SMC	Generally comprehensive treatmentof costs but details of individual salaries missing (resolved through interviews)
Content analysis of 1 year's-worth of paper files – 207 cases	Identification of levels of activity on cases by mediators and involvement of other agencies	Under-reporting of activity. Resolved through analysis of additional detailed records kept by one mediator (48 cases)
Interrogation of SMC housing database of cases handled in one year – 249 cases	Identification of levels of activity on cases by mediators and total time devoted to each case	Breakdown by individual activities not possible
Interviews with mediators	Identification of their allocation of time to a variety of tasks, their working hours and salary levels	Various tasks carried out simultaneously – made it difficult to attribute costs
Study of housing officers' handling of disputesconducted by Dignan *et al.* 1996	To facilitate comparison of costs of mediation and traditional complaint management	

SMC funding and organisational costs

9.7   SMC is one of the largest community mediation centres in the country. It has an annual income of over £150,000, almost double the average found by Dignan *et al.* (1996) in their research on 28 UK community mediation centres. In that study, only five of the centres that responded to their survey had an annual income of over £50,000. It is clear that many of the centres included in Dignan *et al.*'s study relied heavily on volunteers with the result that their income gives few clues as to real costs. It can be seen from table 9.2 that in the three-year period from 1995-8, SMC received grants and donations totalling £463,615, from a variety of sources. The majority (88 per cent) of this income was generated through grants and donations from borough, city or county councils (£406,945 in three years). This amount is double the proportion (42 per cent) generated by the 28 centres in Dignan *et al.*'s (1996) study. Those organisations relied more on national charities (17 per cent) and central government grants (17 per cent) for their funding, although such grants are more likely to cover discrete projects than general running costs of community mediation programmes. The main source of SMC's income is service-level agreements with departments within the London Borough of Southwark. In return for a block grant the Centre accepts a set number of referrals from various named departments. The size of other grants and donations ranged from £100 up to £10,000.

Table 9.2 Sources of funding

	1995/6	1996/7	1997/8	Total	
Borough/City/County Councils	125019	136408	145518	406945	88.0%
Housing Associations	0	600	0	600	0.1%
Mediation Agencies	0	900	0	900	0.1%
Training	1150	0	13312	14462	3.0%
Regional Grants	12500	297	0	12797	3.0%
Other Grants*	5168	12858	1000	19026	4.0%
Miscellaneous	390	5049	3446	8885	2.0%
Total	144227	156112	163276	463615	100.0%

* Including Peabody Foundation, Price Waterhouse, Goldsmiths Trust, Calouste Gulbenkian Foundation and the French Protestant Church in London.

SMC overhead costs

9.8   How does SMC use the funding it receives? In the sections which follow we consider their overheads, costs associated with individual mediator activity and how the data reviewed can be used to compute the costs of cases. Untypically, SMC does not make extensive use of volunteer mediators. Instead, it employs six full-time members of staff to mediate[1], manage referrals and administer the Centre. In addition to six trained mediators, it has a full-time administrator and, at the time of the study, eight trained volunteers. Thus, the majority of the Centres' expenditure[2] goes towards salaries (£114,530 or 75 per cent) and associated costs such as national insurance contributions and pension schemes (£13,212 or nine per cent). This makes the average total annual expenditure on staff £127,742 (83 per cent of the Centre's total expenditure). Dignan *et al.* (1996) found that only 20 of the 28 services included in their study incurred costs under this category and of those that did their average total expenditure on salaries was 66 per cent of total income. Table 9.3 presents details of their expenditure over time.

Table 9.3 Southwark Mediation Centre expenditure

Fixed costs	1995/96		1996/97		1997/98	
Administration costs	5599	(4%)	6260	(4%)	11238	(7%)
Rent and rates	4016	(3%)	5297	(3%)	6537	(4%)
Telephone	2590	(2%)	3490	(2%)	3320	(2%)
Audit and accountancy	490	(0%)	559	(0%)	591	(0%)
Depreciation	710	(0%)	989	(1%)	1043	(1%)
Insurance	871	(1%)	701	(0%)	582	(0%)
Staff advertising	1181	(1%)	759	(0%)	208	(0%)
Bank charges and interest	149	(0%)	175	(0%)	111	(0%)
Publicity	491	(0%)	206	(0%)	0	(0%)
Variable costs						
Salaries/wages	110179	(77%)	117565	(76%)	115847	(71%)
Employer's NIC	9910	(7%)	10544	(7%)	10128	(6%)
School project expenses	1230	(1%)	0	(0%)	4000	(2%)
Training and conference fees	788	(1%)	1090	(1%)	3185	(2%)
Pension costs	2763	(2%)	4207	(3%)	2086	(1%)
Travel	1735	(1%)	1285	(1%)	1923	(1%)
Expenses	190	(0%)	12	(0%)	865	(1%)
Refreshments and hospitality	364	(0%)	809	(1%)	740	(0%)
Meeting rooms	206	(0%)	600	(0%)	80	(0%)
Total	**143462**	**(100%)**	**154548**	**(100%)**	**162484**	**(100%)**

Percentages below 0.5% have all been rounded down to 0 in this table.

9.9   When variable costs which are related to individual projects are excluded (training and conference fees, refreshments and hospitality, travel, expenses and school project expenses) the fixed overhead for 1997/8 can be calculated as £23,710 which is 15 per cent of total expenditure. Excluding salaries and associated costs, variable costs amount to £10,713[3] for 1997/8.

Time spent by mediators on general and specific tasks

9.10   The data presented in table 9.3 show that expenditure on mediators' salaries is by far the largest consideration in our cost analysis. In this section, we identify how mediators spend their time at SMC and how their activities can be translated into costs. To assess accurately the cost of dispute management, it is first necessary to distinguish between the salaried costs associated with case management and the salaried costs associated with more general duties related to dispute management.

9.11   General duties carried out by mediators fall into a number of categories such as fund-raising, public relations and training of SMC volunteers and staff from other agencies. A considerable amount of time is also spent generating case referrals from the agencies with which they have a service agreement. Dignan *et al.* (1996) describe community mediators as 'jacks of all trades' and our interviews and observations of the Centre confirm this. In addition to managing disputes, they carry out a variety of tasks which are essential for the existence of the Centre. The first section of table 9.4 details the time that mediators estimated they spend in an average month[4] on these general tasks. This reveals the difference in the balance of work between the co-ordinator and other mediators. Predictably, the co-ordinator spends more time on training and supervising staff.

9.12   How long do mediators spend on casework? Table 9.5 shows how much time mediators spend on managing specific disputes. It reveals that, despite the pressures on mediators to generate new work and income, the bulk of their time is spent on case orientated tasks. The percentage of time that project workers can devote to specific case management tasks averages at around 76 per cent - shuttle mediation, talking to parties on the phone and face-to-face mediation are the most time-consuming activities of the mediators. Looking at tables 9.4 and 9.5 together, it can be seen that the remaining time that project workers have is mostly spent on general SMC-related duties, such as referral-generating tasks (eight per cent), giving talks and presentations (five per cent), chasing referrals (five per cent) and providing reports (three per cent).

Table 9.4 Breakdown of general mediator tasks by individual mediators in hours (% in brackets)

General tasks connected to running SMC

	Co-ordinator		Project worker 1		Project worker 2		Assistant co-ordinator & project worker	
preparing for and going to staff meetings	3	(2)	4	(3)	2	(1)	3	(2)
attending courses and conferences	3	(2)	0	(0)	0	(0)	6	(4)
giving talks/presentations to other agencies	3	(2)	4.5	(3)	3	(2)	8	(5)
office time (filing)	2	(1)	6	(4)	5	(4)	2	(1)
chasing referrals	1	(1)	6	(4)	4	(3)	7	(4)
preparing reports for agencies	0.5	(0*)	1.5	(1)	3.5	(3)	5	(3)
supervision meetings	5	(3)	0.5	(0*)	1	(1)	3	(2)
supervising volunteers	1	(1)	1	(1)	0	(0)	1	(1)
dealing with casual enquiries	1	(1)	1	(1)	2	(1)	2	(1)
negotiating funding	1	(1)	0	(0)	0	(0)	2	(1)
income generating	4.5	(3)	0	(0)	0	(0)	6	(4)
training	10	(7)	0	(0)	0	(0)	10	(6)
lunch breaks/tea breaks	1	(1)	12	(8)	2	(1)	4	(3)
Total	**36**	**(24)**	**36.5**	**(23)**	**22.5**	**(16)**	**59**	**(24)**

9.13 A number of tasks identified are carried out simultaneously. For instance, talking to a housing officer about a specific case, presents mediators with the opportunity to enquire after other potential referrals. Additionally, lunch and tea breaks often coincide with keeping records and discussion of cases with colleagues. Mediators also indicated that they would often update records as they were speaking to clients on the telephone and that individual case discussion would occur during supervision meetings.

9.14 How long do mediators spend on individual cases? Elsewhere in this report, we have detailed the average time taken to perform certain tasks associated with mediation, such as visits, letter-writing and phone calls (see chapter 6). In addition, we were able to use other sources of data to identify the amount of time spent on cases. The content analysis of one year's-worth of paper files (207 cases) on cases referred to the Centre, interrogation of the SMC database (249 cases) and detailed reports on time management by one of the mediators at the Centre (48 cases) were also used in our calculations. As we have already indicated (see table

Table 9.5 Breakdown of specific mediator tasks by individual mediators in hours (% in brackets)

Specific tasks connected with cases

inputting and keeping records	4	(3)	3	(2)	15	(11)	10	(6)
talking to colleagues about cases	13	(9)	18	(12)	10	(7)	12	(8)
writing letters to parties	7	(5)	8	(5)	7	(5)	6	(4)
speaking to parties on the telephone	30	(20)	24	(15)	20	(14)	20	(13)
visiting parties in home (shuttle mediation)	28	(19)	24	(15)	30	(21)	30	(19)
travelling (visits)	10	(7)	16	(10)	7	(5)	8	(5)
face-to-face mediation	16	(11)	6	(4)	8	(6)	5	(3)
waiting for parties	1	(1)	0.5	(0*)	0.5	(0*)	2	(1)
Total	**112**	**(76)**	**119.5**	**(77)**	**117.5**	**(84)**	**101**	**(63)**

*In these cases 0.3% of the mediator's time was spent on these tasks. However, these figures were rounded down for the sake of consistency within the table.

9.1) there was some concern that entries on the paper files under-estimated levels of activity. For these reasons we have relied on the other two sources of data which we found produced similar statistics. Analysis of these datasets revealed that mediators spent on average a total of between five hours (individual mediator data[5]) and 4.75 hours (housing database) on each case. The housing database also revealed that the total time spent on cases ranged from six minutes to 16 hours.

What are the costs associated with mediation activities?

9.15   The time spent on the tasks identified in tables 9.4 and 9.5 can also be expressed in financial terms. This is possible because data were collected on working hours, salaries and general overheads. Costs can be presented as general overhead costs and specific case costs or as a combination of these two types. In the first part of this section, we present the annual costs to SMC of both general and specific tasks. In the second part, we use these data to assess the cost of mediating individual cases, taking into account the general or overhead costs identified in table 9.3 above, and the costs of carrying out specific management tasks.

9.16   Despite their different levels of seniority, mediators at the Centre command similar net salaries within the range of £20-22,000 (excluding National Insurance and other contributions). Because of this similarity, we have calculated and used an average gross salary of £23,783[6] (including NI contributions and pension costs paid by the Centre). Table 9.6 translates the estimated time spent on the various tasks completed by staff into total financial costs to the Centre.

Table 9.6 Breakdown of mediator tasks in an average month

General tasks connected to running SMC	Average hours in a month spent on task	Percentage of time spent on task	Average cost based on average salary £*
training	5.00	3	713
lunch breaks/tea breaks	4.75	3	713
giving talks/presentations to other agencies	4.63	3	713
chasing referrals	4.50	3	713
office time (filing)	3.75	2	476
preparing for and going to staff meetings	3.00	2	476
income generating	2.63	2	476
preparing reports for agencies	2.63	2	476
supervision meetings	2.38	2	476
attending courses and conferences	2.25	1	238
dealing with casual enquiries	1.50	1	238
negotiating funding	0.75	0.5	119
supervising volunteers	0.75	0.5	119
Total	**38.50**	**25**	**5946**
Specific tasks connected with cases			
visiting parties in home (shuttle mediation)	28.00	19	4519
speaking to parties on the telephone	23.50	16	3805
talking to colleagues about cases	13.25	9	2140
speaking to referring agency about cases	12.75	8	1903
travelling (visits)	10.25	7	1664
face-to-face mediation	8.75	6	1427
inputting and keeping records	8.00	5	1189
writing letters to parties	7.00	5	1189
waiting for parties	1.00	1	238
Total	**112.50**	**76**	**18,074**
		Total for table	24020**

* Based on average salary, National Insurance contributions and pension scheme contributions. On average, SMC employees work 151 hours over four weeks which costs SMC £23,783 annually.

** An additional £237 accounts for rounding up of percentages.

9.17   The total costs of mediators carrying out general duties range from £1277 to £3832. The general tasks which consume 27 per cent of the mediators'[7] time cost the Centre £34,488 annually.

9.18   The annual costs associated with the time that mediators spend on management of individual cases can be seen in figure 9.1. The total costs of carrying out specific tasks range from £1277 to £24,271 annually. Significantly, given the prominence devoted to it in much of the literature on mediation, face-to-face mediation represents just eight per cent (£7665) of the total annual direct costs of £98,362[8]. Individually, mediators spent approximately six per cent of their time on face-to-face mediation translating to costs of approximately £1400. The largest proportion (19 per cent) of salaried time is spent on visiting disputing parties in their homes and speaking to them on the telephone (15 per cent). This represents over £8300 of each mediator's salary.

Figure 9.1 Total annual costs per mediator by task

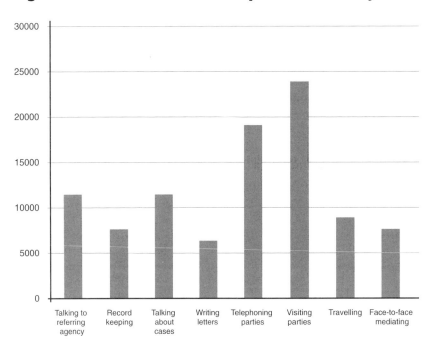

What is the total cost of individual cases?

9.19 From the data presented above, three major categories of costs relating to mediation emerge.

- The costs of tasks relating to specific case tasks, such as visiting the parties, writing letters and making telephone calls. We have shown above that this takes up 76 per cent of mediators' time (see table 9.6)

- The costs of other more general mediator tasks, such as generation of case load through liaising with housing officers, preparing statistical returns which takes up 25 per cent of mediators' time (see table 9.6).

- The organisational costs of running SMC. These include fixed overheads, such as rent and rates, and variable overheads, such as travel and conference fees (see table 9.3).

9.20 When working out the average total cost of case management, all three costs need to be taken into account if costing is to reflect both the direct and indirect costs of mediation. This is because the general tasks undertaken make the specific tasks possible. Table 9.7 shows the breakdown of costs according to the headings identified in paragraph 9.19. These costs have been based on averages, and reflect the Centre's costs for the 1997/8 period.

Table 9.7 Case costs and cost per employee 1997/98 (Housing, ES and Five Estates)

| | Specific case tasks | General mediator tasks | Organisational costs | | |
			Fixed*	Variable	Total
Case†	£225.79	£75.26	£73.17	£36.26	£410.48
Year	£17837.25	£5945.75	£5780.40‡	£2864.20*	£32427.60

Costs associated with mediator time spent on tasks (inc. salary, NIC and pension)

Costs associated with overheads and running

* There were some difficulties in calculating the overhead to be attributed to housing, ES and 5 Estates cases as the Centre also ran a schools project during this period which drew on organisational resources. We have estimated that one of five mediators employed in 1997 spent 75 per cent of their time on the school project and calculated overheads by attaching them to individuals. This allows us to discount 75 per cent of the overheads generated by the schools' project worker in funding costs relating to ES, housing and Five Estates.

† This is based on new 79 cases per project worker, allowing for overlap in case work and projects.

‡ This has been divided by five (mediators) and does not include the administrator as these costs are taken on by each mediator.

9.21 Table 9.6 reveals that just over half (£225.79) of the average cost of individual cases to SMC is made up of specific case management tasks. It includes the other financial costs to SMC that result from their involvement in neighbour disputes. This provides valuable data on the real costs of mediation which have been hidden in studies of organisations who make more extensive use of volunteers.

Assessing the wider costs of neighbour disputes

9.22 The wider costs of neighbour disputes are far reaching and it was difficult within the research remit to try and produce an exhaustive list of them. Many are unquantifiable and indirect. Even where disputes have a direct financial cost to someone, these can also be hard to quantify. Throughout this study we have attempted to trace all aspects of costs and found that three core groups carry the burden of neighbour disputes. These are individuals' costs, agency costs and social or collective costs. The final section of this chapter attempts to draw on the experience of the present research to identify the wider costs of disputes. One dispute may trigger all the costs listed below others may remain contained and not produce the ripple effect that develops.

Agency costs

9.23 As previously mentioned, disputes are referred to SMC at various stages and although some may be referred after the initial dispute is reported to one of the front-line agencies, our interviews and analysis of case files suggest that some preliminary work is carried out on all cases prior to their referral. Housing officers, in particular, invest considerable amounts of time in understanding the issues in dispute, making initial enquiries, writing letters in response and referring cases to appropriate agencies. Many other agencies may also be approached to help neighbours resolve their disputes such as MIND, Age Concern, Citizen's Advice Bureaux. This means that a range of specialist agencies, including SMC, may become involved in dispute management. The true cost of any neighbour dispute depends on the number of agencies that become involved in the resolution process and on the individual costs associated with each agency.

Costs to the individual and society

9.24 The costs to individuals that involve state agencies when in dispute, as we have seen during this study, are mostly unquantifiable. Although some disputants may seek legal advice, this has not been widely used in many of the disputes that we have seen. As the local authority is the most common landlord in these disputes most repairs to properties are carried out free of charge. The direct financial costs to individuals arise through the time that is invested in the resolution of the dispute (such as any time that is spent talking to agencies and writing letters) and the cost of replacing or repairing personal property and goods damaged as a consequence of the dispute. The 'personal' costs to individuals arise both directly and indirectly as a result of a dispute and may generate financial costs. A number of emotional and psychological effects, such as stress and anxiety, as a direct consequence of a dispute were witnessed on several occasions during visits with mediators to disputants' homes. On several occasions parties could not compose themselves whilst describing their dispute and many were tearful during their accounts to the mediators. Other disputants were extremely angry and enraged when giving their accounts. Clearly, these experiences may have a knock-on effect in terms of use of medical services and poor performance at work. Some disputants revealed that their health had been effected by their dispute. Many had needed some medical assistance, ranging from sleeping aids to anti-depressant medication, as a direct result of their dispute. Lack of sleep was cited as a problem in numerous cases and has been recognised as a wider health issue in the local health authority's *Annual Report* (Lambeth, Southwark and Lewisham Health Authority 1997) as a direct consequence of nuisance neighbours.

Conclusion

9.25   Along with other researchers, we have found the cost of mediation difficult to compute. There are several reasons for this. Firstly, many of the costs that are associated with neighbour disputes are unquantifiable and therefore can only be hinted at as a real cost to someone involved. Secondly, when looking at mediation alone it has been difficult to measure the costs that may have been incurred before SMC involvement. Thirdly, when costs are looked at from SMC's involvement, independently from other agencies involvement, it becomes clear that there are direct and indirect case management costs as well as fixed and variable organisational costs that need to be taken into account. Where the difficulty lies with this analysis is that these costs are not mutually exclusive and one may occur to a greater or lesser extent depending on another. With all these points in mind, we have attempted to identify where the real costs of mediation lie and what these have been on average over the 1997/8 period. Future research could valuably compare the costs of mediation with those of traditional dispute management in more detail. Throughout this report we have been able to identify the potential for double handling of disputes, the extra work involved when cases are referred on as mature disputes and the various stages at which they might be referred. But each of these topics deserves revisiting. Despite these caveats we have produced data which we hope will be of benefit in quantifying the real costs associated with a properly funded organisation. The data are important if the access to justice reforms heralded by Lord Woolf are to involve more than the public sector relying on the services of mediators who give their time for free as volunteers.

Endnotes

1. Although, by the end of this evaluation SMC had additional members of staff, these costs are based on six members of staff that were employed during this project.

2. Figures are based on averages over three years from 1995-8.

3. This includes £4000 associated with the schools project.

4. Based on an average four-week period

5. The time spent on visits has been doubled as mediators always go on visits with another mediator. Until recently, the co-mediator has also been a salaried member of staff.

6. The co-ordinator of the Centre was keen that individual salaries were not made public. This method allows us to provide a veneer of confidentiality.

7. Including the co-ordinator.

8. This and the total for general costs exceeds the estimated annual expenditure on wages due to percentages being rounded off and translations being taken to the decimal point.

Chapter 10: Conclusion

Introduction

10.1 During the course of this report, we have examined a number of issues which will be of interest to policy makers, academics and practitioners. The data and arguments have been presented in such a way as to attempt to engage with all three audiences. Each of these groups has their own story of the successes of community mediation as well as concerns about its development and growth. The data reported are suggestive of a number of claims about mediation, some of which are conflicting and confusing. Undoubtedly, some of our findings will prove unpalatable to those who are interested in hearing definitive answers to questions about the successes or failures of community mediation. We hope that the value of the report is that it attempts to revisit these themes and in doing so bring new insights and pose new questions by reference to empirical data. Many of the claims of the mediation movement have been overly ambitious and much mediation occurs in the shadow and under the influence of formal law rather than as an alternative to it. But, the overall thrust of this report is that mediation, nonetheless, has the potential to re-construct disputes in a way which assigns more power to disputants and most importantly shifts the focus away from individual grievances towards the situational factors which give rise to grievances in poor and deprived inner-city boroughs.

10.2 In part, this report serves the function of muddying the waters in a debate in which accounts of the value of mediation have become polarised and overly simplistic. Critics of mediation have focused their concerns on the inability of community mediation to reach out to whole communities; its lack of success in reducing state control and empowering individuals; its tendency to reinforce existing inequalities between disputants; and mediators' over-emphasis on the value of peace and harmony. Mediation 'evangelists' have been equally as strident in their claims that mediation can empower people and communities, reduce the power of the state over the lives of its citizenry and educate disputants in life skills. These opposing claims are useful to the extent that they provide a set of extreme opposites and a template of issues against which to interpret the data collected for the study reported here.

10.3 Intensive debate about the value of community mediation has only served to entrench positions. Academic researchers bear some of the responsibility for this state of affairs. In her discussion of the intellectual stalemate reached Cain (1988) has argued:

> *Academic criticism and negative evaluation have created a growing chorus of despair, a feeling that the devil of formal justice may, after all, be better than his dangerously unfamiliar informal brother. This chorus is occasionally punctuated by an attenuated left-wing squeak of hope that by some dialectical feat a 'genuinely' human and popular form of justice may emerge in spite of all from this newly identified diabolical situation. (p.51)*

10.4 At the same time, the trend towards simplistic accounts of mediation has been encouraged by the fervour with which policy makers are attempting to divert disputes away from the courts and formal processes. Increasing interest in alternative disputes resolution has provided an unprecedented opportunity for practitioners to promote mediation to responsive policy audiences. Mediation is receiving more attention than ever before. But, in turn, these developments have created an environment in which it is difficult to encourage caution and evidence-based practice.

10.5 It is clear that research on mediation has not always been well received by policy makers or practitioners. Tensions exist between the various groups with an interest in community mediation. Those who are disposed to believe that mediation can save costs and those who believe that it produces better quality outcomes see the stories of only partial success of mediation as a threat. Moreover, the political gains made by mediators in capturing the imagination of policy makers can all too easily be undermined by negative or ambivalent academic critiques of the process. Despite these constraints it is a basic tenet of this report that the claims and rhetoric of those committed to mediation must be tested and challenged before we are able to determine whether mediation is of benefit to disputants and communities as well as mediators and policy makers. This report represents a modest attempt to encourage reflection about the possibilities of mediation and its limitations.

The 'problem' of neighbour disputes

10.6 Some commentators have suggested that disputes between neighbours are becoming a significant social problem and this has fuelled debate about the need for different approaches to the problem. They have hinted at the ways in which such disputes reflect the development of an increasingly dysfunctional society. National statistics appear to reflect this trend. There have been significant increases in the number of reported noise-related disputes and research has drawn attention to the increase in the amount of time that housing officers devote to dealing with such problems. Concerns about the increasing incidence of neighbours' disputes have been paralleled by concerns about the costs of managing them. In the social housing sector, the expense of dealing with neighbourhood conflict falls on housing offices but a number of other state funded agencies may also become embroiled such as the NHS, social services and the police. In some quarters these concerns have led to the suggestion that the problem of neighbour disputes is becoming something of a crisis and these fears have paved the way for reform. To date, there have been two policy responses to this analysis which approach the problem from very different perspectives. Firstly, more and more councils are looking to mediation agencies to help them resolve disputes in a more conciliatory manner in the hope that they will not escalate. Secondly, new and more coercive legal powers have been introduced for councils charged with responsibility for managing and resolving disputes between social tenants.

10.7 Despite the construction of the problem as a crisis, research suggests that the claims that neighbour disputes pose an increasing problem to our social order and court system have to be examined closely. Our research has demonstrated that only a minority of neighbour disputes are ever managed through the courts and that most disputants fail to pursue their grievance against a neighbour once it has been lodged as a formal complaint. Recent research by Genn (1999) supports these data and provides further evidence of the tendency for people to put up with their problems. Her study demonstrates that the majority of those experiencing problems with their neighbour respond by either living with the problem or approaching their neighbour direct. Both datasets suggest that, rather than being seen as a reflection of a dysfunctional society, disputes between neighbours which are referred to housing offices are best viewed as an atypical response to conflict within society. Dignan *et al.* (1996) have also suggested that the apparent upturn in the official recording of complaints about neighbours does no more than reflect new reporting systems.

Putting the research in context

10.8 The use of mediation in neighbourhood disputes in Southwark cannot be understood in isolation. Many of the problems experienced by Southwark residents may be alien to those living in more rural settings. Levels of deprivation are extremely high in the borough and the stresses of high rise inner-city life undoubtedly provide a backdrop against which many of the disputes between neighbours arise. Southwark is also a borough in the process of change. Work is being done to alleviate the problems caused by poor housing conditions and lack of privacy and government and EU grants are funding much of this regeneration. There is an increased emphasis on a move from high to low density housing and on the importance of re-building a sense of community.

10.9 The re-generation of the borough has provided many opportunities for SMC to increase its activity and income, an opportunity which has been readily embraced. The operational model they have adopted is radically different from most community mediation centres which have little core funding and continue to rely on volunteer mediators. The result has been that the Centre is now one of the largest in the country and handles many more disputes than is the norm. The increased level of funding has also facilitated its mediators becoming involved in an array of different projects ranging from neighbour disputes to those involving criminal offenders and children. One of the undoubted successes of the Centre is the way in which staff have been given a greater sense of job security. All staff talked of their personal growth and their increasing pride in the efficiency of service delivery. Despite these developments they only hesitantly accepted our suggestion that they were becoming increasing professionalised because of the suggestion it brought with it that this meant that they were moving away from their 'community' roots.

10.10 Despite the diversity of its funding arrangements, SMC remains highly reliant on money from Southwark Council. The type of funding generated means that they are heavily dependent on housing officers for referral of cases to them. They have worked hard to maintain their independence but their attempts to generate referrals mean that they inevitably strive towards establishing a good working relationship with a handful of housing officers. Rather than being a cause for concern, mediators in the study argued that the emphasis on getting housing officers to trust them increased the influence they could have on the provision of services in favour of tenants.

10.11 These data suggest that community mediators are not necessarily entirely autonomous from council or state legality or completely encompassed by it. Fitzpatrick (1992) claims that the two domains are mutually constitutive social fields that affect one another's historical identities. Thus, each depends on the presence of the other, and the difference between them, to formulate their identity. According to this line of thought, community mediation can have embedded and unembedded elements. Pavlich (1996a) argues that community mediation is a related political development to the state which nonetheless had developed with a political rationality of its own. Through this analysis we are able to conceive of a form of 'governmentality' fostered by such movements as community mediation which exists outside of, but draws on, the state.

The shadow of the law

10.12 As a result of these funding arrangements, housing officers have become pivotal in the process of referring cases and operate as gatekeepers to both mediation and the legal process. Our research suggests that most are reluctant to send more than a handful of cases to SMC, although this still amounts to many more referrals per annum than are dealt with by other community mediation services.

Significantly, housing officers were equally reluctant to use the more formal legal powers granted to them in recent legislation. These powers are extensive but rarely used to initiate litigation. Litigation is viewed as burdensome and housing officers have a strong preference for internal management of disputes between neighbours.

10.13   Whilst management of the majority of cases within the housing office may be an economically efficient way of dealing with cases, it is clear that disposal rather than resolution is more often their goal. Housing officers have considerable success in closing cases without referring them to mediation or the legal services department of the Council. However, their approach is far from conciliatory and they make considerable use of the threat of eviction. Once a complaint has been made by one tenant, disputants are commonly asked to attend the office to discuss the problem. In some cases, where the source of the dispute can be managed by instigating repairs or alterations to the properties involved, then this may be done. But in the majority of cases discussions with the disputants are followed by a formal letter in which eviction is threatened if a breach of the tenancy agreement can be found. Not surprisingly, such letters are sufficient to silence most disputants.

10.14   Use of the threat of eviction makes clear the huge inequality of bargaining power between the council and social tenants. When a complainant is supported by the power of the State to evict a tenant the management of the dispute is rightly labelled coercive. Against this backdrop mediators are able to make a convincing case for providing an alternative to formal handling of the dispute by state officials. But, somewhat paradoxically, it also means that mediation is conducted in the shadow of such coercive powers. Many of the disputants who take part in mediation have already received a letter reminding them of the council's power to evict. Rather than empowering disputants this could have the effect of encouraging them to take a passive or conciliatory role in dispute resolution. Moreover, some housing officers argued that because referral to mediation suggested that the council has made a serious attempt to resolve the dispute in a reasonable manner, it could aid their attempt to pursue use of their coercive powers through the courts. In this sense, mediation becomes one part of the state machinery of law enforcement rather than an alternative to it.

A promising development?

10.15   Despite this backdrop, proponents of mediation have argued that it has a number of benefits over and above the more coercive formal methods of resolving used by the council and legal system. As interest in mediation has increased there has been a significant growth in the number of community mediation centres, especially in the inner cities. A close examination of the mediation 'movement' suggests that it has an ideological rationality rather than a homogenous identity. Despite this, supporters of mediation argue that what differentiates it from other forms of dispute resolution is that it is less coercive and focuses on the importance of the empowerment of individuals through informal and accessible processes which are governed by the disputants. Mediation's ability to restore peace and involve residents in building functioning communities have also been stressed. Interviews with housing officers and disputants presented in this report suggest that there is considerable satisfaction amongst users of SMC's mediation services with the process of mediation once cases are referred. In part, this is because difficult cases could be diverted away from housing offices but housing officers also suggested that the better quality outcomes could be achieved because mediators had more time to unravel the causes of the dispute and listen to full accounts of disputants' grievances.

10.16 The success of mediation cannot be determined by reference to the number of settlements reached alone. The data collected for this study show that the agency's 'capture' of cases referred to it is incomplete either because the parties choose not to engage with mediators or because disputes are referred when the parties have become too entrenched. For the majority of cases referred to the agency, mediation is not required. There are high levels of unseen work undertaken by mediators in processing cases. The time devoted to cases does not necessarily increase as they move towards shuttle or face-to-face mediation. In fact, the incidence of contact with the parties may be more frequent where mediation is not pursued. This finding has implications for costing the services of the agency as costs have to be spread across all cases and not just those which are mediated.

10.17 As it has grown and undergone structural re-organisation, staff have also been encouraged to re-consider their own approach to mediation. Much of their development has occurred in a vacuum, without reference to academic debate or national debate amongst mediation centres. This goes some way to explaining the slight antipathy they have towards having a dominant model of mediation imposed upon them. Data collected on the processing of cases demonstrate that SMC mediators structure their case management in a different way from that anticipated by literature in the field. Firstly, significant use is made of the telephone as a way of engaging the parties and visiting the issues in the dispute. Secondly, the parties are much more likely to experience shuttle mediation than the face-to-face variety. Thirdly, rather than being seen as a discrete event mediation is more appropriately viewed as a process which can take place through face-to-face contact, telephone conversations or visits to the home.

10.18 The Centre's preference for shuttle mediation is a relatively recent development and reflects their concerns that many disputants do not want to meet face to face. Even where the parties are prepared to meet, mediators argued that the interaction might be too volatile for it to be feasible. Mediators in the study actively encouraged reliance on the shuttle approach and they tended to take a strong lead on the choice between these two options. Critics of mediation have been concerned that such controls of process pose a strong challenge to the ideological framework within which the majority of community mediators seek to operate. Commentators have claimed that they can be seen as a form of manipulation because the management of the time and space in which discussion occurs is interconnected with a manipulation of the substance of the discussion and regulation of the parties' participation. By not exposing the parties to each other there is a fear that there are fewer opportunities for them to challenge each other's accounts in a way which allows them, rather than the mediator, to set the agenda. There is a sense in which the practice encourages the construction of the notion of a 'good disputant' who contains their anger and violent tendencies. The emphasis here, as in more formal state-sanctioned arenas, is on the restoration of order.

10.19 But data collected for the study also suggest that mediators at Southwark are prepared to challenge the somewhat slavish devotion to the idea of neutrality and impartiality which remains so cherished by other members of the community mediation 'movement'. For some writers the constant reference to the possibility of neutrality and impartiality is just one way for mediators to gain respectability in the eyes of policy makers accustomed to court based notions of procedural justice. Mediators in the study suggested that for them the goal of neutrality and non-partisanship espoused by mediation gurus might not be appropriate or attainable. The possibility of re-visiting the value of an unyielding commitment to neutrality is attractive.

10.20 Expectations of neutrality cause particular problems in a community setting. Community mediators are chosen from the community in which they manage disputes because of their ability to empathise, assimilate and remain sensitive to the needs of local residents. In this sense they are chosen because of their partisanship. While neutrality may be aspired to when dealing with disputes between neighbours, the aspiration loses its point when the dispute reveals the dereliction of a duty by the state as a social landlord. The mediators being evaluated in this study not only admitted of the impossibility of neutrality, they also have concerns about the relevance of neutrality in such situation.

10.21 These data go some way to addressing the major concern of critics that mediation and other informal methods of disputes resolution have tended to ape formal state law and adopt many of the same rituals and customs. The fact that mediators in this study talked about 'stepping out of role' reflects that traditional boundaries as to what is considered good mediation practice still strongly influence their practice. But their approach to occasional advice giving also suggests that neutrality is not always an appropriate goal where there is an underlying problem which they believe needs resolution. Southwark mediators have demonstrated that, when they think that help is what is needed, pragmatism is as attractive as idealism.

Re-constructing disputes

10.22 In their sessions with disputants mediators claim to help the parties unravel the nature of their grievance and the causes of it. The data presented in this report suggest that they also help the parties to translate and re-construct the dispute. Most notably, they are prepared to admit the part they play in raising some disputants' awareness of the role the state has in creating the conditions which make disputes more likely. In this way the tendency for mediation to individualise disputes by concentrating on the accounts and needs of the individuals effected is muted. Moreover, the role of the state as a neutral funder of private dispute resolution is also challenged when they are identified as one of the parties with some responsibility for what has happened.

10.23 The state's role in prompting disputes was recognised by both mediators and housing officers. Recognition of the situational factors which lead to disputes such as poor insulation and the stress caused by high-rise living shifts the emphasis away from the individualisation of blame and management of disputes as discrete activities towards the attribution of responsibility to more pervasive conditions. Outside of the context of individual mediations, mediators in the study were also occasionally prepared to convey the collective concerns of residence about poor housing conditions to state officials In this way they acted as advocates for some members of the community. It was also clear from the data that by managing the expectations of residents about the standard of service which it was feasible for the council to deliver they were prepared to convey messages in the opposite direction as well.

10.24 We suggest that the ways in which the mediation agency being evaluated interacted with the council and local community provides an example of how partnerships between the public and voluntary sector can be formulated and managed. In particular, the data address the concerns of some critics, that rather than offering an alternative to state management of disputes, mediators become mere agents of state organisations who process cases on their behalf. Pavlich (1996a) summed up this viewpoint when he suggested of those involved in the debate that:

> *They have, in short, narrowed the debate on community mediation to an exploration of the extent to which it expands and/or intensifies state control. In the process, sustained analyses of community mediation as possibly harbouring elements that are not embedded in state control, or functional for the latter, are not placed on critical agendas. (p.713)*

10.25 The data presented in this report suggests that the situation is actually much more complex. We do not seek to deny the somewhat inevitable close links between state-funded mediation services and state agencies. However, the data we have presented also suggest that, as well as resolving the disputes of neighbours, mediators are prepared to act as go-betweens, bearing messages from and to groups and state agencies. Instead of viewing them as neutral or independent, this allows them to be seen, more realistically, as embedded in both communities and with interests in both. The claim that mediation has the potential to restructure or change whole communities may be an ambitious one but our data suggest that neighbour conflicts provide important contextual material which can facilitate some improvement and change within communities. The changes brought about by message bearing and advocacy are much more modest everyday changes than those called for by left wing critics of mediation who are concerned that it suppresses collective political consciousness amongst the disadvantaged. It may not have the potential to deal with disputes and rebuild communities but mediation can effect some change on levels of consciousness and allow residents to put forward different approaches to the issues raised in disputes from those recognised by the council.

In closing ...

10.26 This chapter has reviewed the major arguments to have emerged from this report. It has suggested that the claims of proponents of mediation remain attractive but that the possibility of them becoming reality has been undermined by debate about the nature of the relationship between the state, agencies and individuals, formalism and informalism, the empowered and disempowered. Despite these concerns, even the most vocal critics of community mediation have found it hard to deny the plausibility of all aspects of the community mediation project and the possibilities for improvements in the provision of state-sanctioned justice it suggests. A major conclusion of this report has been the need to move away from conception of dispute resolution procedures as being inside and outside of the state to a more realistic evaluation of exactly how the socio-legal dynamics of partnerships with the state are played out in practice.

10.27 Whilst remaining cautious of the inflated and often evangelical claims of proponents of mediation, we would argue that community mediation has considerable potential. It may not be able to restructure communities in ways which privilege the residents of an area over state agencies, but this is not surprising. Residents of inner-city boroughs such as Southwark have an intense and intimate relationship with state agencies. But mediation can have a very discernible impact on the quality of dispute resolution when the activities of mediators are compared to the management of disputes by housing officers. It allows participants to claw back some of their autonomy from their social landlord. This notion of empowerment may be much more incremental and modest than that anticipated by some, but it remains important to tenants involved in the process.

References

Abel, R L, 'The Contradictions of Informal Justice' in *The Politics of Informal Justice*, R L Abel (ed.), London, Academic Press, 1982.

Adler, P, Lovaas, K and Milner, N, 'The ideologies of mediation: the movement's own story', *Law and Policy* 10(4), 1988, pp. 317-39.

Aldbourne Associates, *Managing Neighbour Complaints in Social Housing*, Aldbourne, Aldbourne Associates, 1993.

Allsop, J, 'Two sides to every story: complainants' and doctors' perspectives in disputes about medical care in a general practice setting', *Law and Policy* 16(2), 1994, pp. 149-84.

Billinghurst, T, 'Mediation UK and its member services' in *Neighbour Disputes: Comparing the cost effectiveness of mediation and alternative approaches*, J Dignan, A Sorsby and J Hibbert (eds), Centre for Criminological and Legal Research, University of Sheffield, 1996.

Black, D and Baumgartner, M, 'Toward a theory of a third party' in *Empirical Theories about Courts*, K Boyum and L Mather (eds), New York, Longman, 1983.

Brown, H and Marriot, A, *ADR Principles and Practice*, London, Sweet and Maxwell, 1993.

Bush, R, 'Efficiency and protection or empowerment and recognition? The mediator's role and ethical standards in mediation', *Florida Law Review* 41, 1989, pp. 253-86.

Bush, R and Folger, J, *The Promise of Mediation – Responding to conflict through empowerment and recognition*, San Francisco, Jossey-Bass, 1994.

Cain, M, 'Beyond informal justice' in *Informal Justice?*, R Mathews (ed.) London, Sage Publications,1988.

Cain, M and Kulcsar, K, 'Thinking disputes: an essay on the origins of the dispute industry', *Law and Society Review* 16, 1982, pp. 375-402.

Caplan, P, 'Anthropology and the study of disputes' in *Understanding Disputes: The politics of argument*, P Caplan (ed.), Oxford, Berg, 1995.

Chartered Institute of Housing, *Complaints about Noise received by Environmental Health Officers*, Social Trends Dataset at http://www.statistics.gov.uk/statbase, 2000.

Colson, E, 'The contentiousness of disputes', *Understanding Disputes: The politics of argument*, in P Caplan (ed.), Oxford, Berg, 1995.

Conciliation Project Unit, *The Costs and Effectiveness of Family Conciliation*, London, Lord Chancellor's Department, 1989.

Damaska, M, *The Faces of Justice and State Authority: A comparative approach to legal process*, New Haven, Yale University Press, 1986.

Davis, G, *Partisans and Mediators: The resolution of divorce disputes*, Oxford, Clarendon Press, 1988.

Davis, G and Roberts, M, *Access to Agreement: A consumer study of mediation in family disputes*, Milton Keynes, Open University Press, 1988.

Delgado, R, Dunn, C, Brown, P, Lee, H. and Hubbert, D, 'Fairness and formality: minimising the risk of prejudice in alternative dispute resolution', *Wisconsin Law Review*, 1985, 1359-404.

Dignan, J, Sorsby, A and Hibbert, J, *Neighbour Disputes: Comparing the cost-effectiveness of mediation and alternative approaches*, Sheffield, Centre for Criminological and Legal Research, University of Sheffield, 1996.

Dingwall, R and Greatbatch, D, 'Who is in charge? Rhetoric and evidence in the study of mediation', *Journal of Social Welfare and Family Law* 17(2), 1993, p9. 199-206.

Du Bow, F. and McEwen, C., 'Community Boards and analytical profile', in *The Possibility of Popular Justice*, Merry and Milner (eds), Michigan, 1996.

Engle-Merry, S. and Milner, N. 'Introduction', in *The Possibility of Popular Justice*, Merry and Milner (eds), Michigan, 1996.

Felstiner, W. and Williams, L., 'Mediation as an alternative to criminal prosecution', *Law and Human Behavior* 2(3), 1978, pp. 233-44.

Fiss, O, 'Against Settlement', *Yale Law Review* 93, 1984, pp. 1073-89.

Fitzpatrick, P., 'The impossibility of popular justice', *Social and Legal Studies: An International Journal* 1, 1992, pp. 199-215.

Fuller, L, 'Mediation - its forms and functions', *Southern California Law Review* 44, 1971, pp. 305-39.

Galanter, M, 'Justice in many rooms: courts, private order and indigenous law', *Journal of Pluralism and Unofficial Law* 19, 1981, pp. 1-25.

General Accident (1995) *Good Neighbours Survey*, Perth, Opinion Business Research.

Genn, H, *Paths to Justice: What people do and think about going to law,* Oxford, Hart, 1999.

Genn, H, *Final Report to the Lord Chancellor on the County Court Pilot Scheme,* London, Lord Chancellor's Department, 1998.

Greatbatch, D and Dingwall, R 'Selective facilitation: some preliminary observations on the strategy used by divorce mediation', *Law and Society Review* 23(4), 1989, 613-41.

Grillo, T., 'The mediation alternative: process dangers for women', *The Yale Law Journal* 100, 1991, pp 1545-610.

Haslam, C, 'Foreword', *Neighbour Disputes: Comparing the cost effectiveness of mediation and alternative approaches,* in J Dignan, A Sorsby and J Hibbert (eds), Sheffield, Centre for Criminological and Legal Research, University of Sheffield, 1996.

Harrington, C, 'Socio-legal concepts in mediation ideology', 1 *Legal Studies Forum* 9(1), 1985, 33-8.

Hofrichter, R, 'Neighbourhood justice and the social control of American capitalism: a perspective' in *The Politics of Informal Justice, Vol. 1: The American Experience,* R Abel (ed.), New York, Academic Press, 1982.

Karn,V, Lickiss, R, Hughes, D and Crawley, J, *Neighbour Disputes: Responses by social landlords,* Coventry, Institute of Housing, 1993.

Knapp, M, 'Principles of applied cost research' in *Costing Community Care: theory and practice*, A Netten and J Beecham (eds), Aldershot, Ashgate, 1993.

Lambeth, Southwark and Lewisham Health Authority, *1996/97 Annual Report of the Director of Public Health*, London, Lambeth, Southwark and Lewisham Health Authority, 1997.

Leibmann, M, 'Community and neighbourhood mediation: a UK perspective' in *Rethinking Disputes: The mediation alternative*, J MacFarlene (ed.), London, Cavendish Publishing, 1997.

Leibmann, M, 'The future of community mediation' in *Achieving Civil Justice: Appropriate dispute resolution for the 1990s*, R Smith (ed.), London, Legal Action Group, 1996.

Levin, A and Golash, D, 'Alternative dispute resolution in federal district courts', *University of Florida Law Review* 37, 1985, pp. 29-59.

Lloyd-Bostock, S and Mulcahy, L, 'The social psychology of making and responding to hospital complaints: an account model of complaint processes', *Law and Policy* 16(2), 1994, 123-48. Also appears in *A Reader on Administrative Law*, D Galligan (ed.), Oxford, Oxford University Press, 1996.

Lord Chancellor's Department, *Access to Justice*, London, HMSO, 1996.

Lord Chancellor's Department, *Access to Justice: Interim Report*, London, HMSO, 1996a.

Mather, L and Ygnvesson, B, 'Language, audience, and the transformation of disputes', *Law and Society Review* 15, 1980-1, pp. 775-822.

Matthews, R, 'Reassessing Informal Justice', in *Informal Justice*, R Matthews (ed.), London, Sage, 1988.

McCarthy, P, Simpson, B, Hill, M and Corlyon, J, *Grievances, Complaints and Local Government*, Aldershot, Avebury, 1992.

Meschievitz, C, 'Mediation and medical malpractie: problems with definition and implementation', *Law and Contemporary Problems* 54(1), 1991, pp. 196-215.

Metzloff, T, 'Alternative dispute resolution strategies in medical malpractice', *Alaska Law Review* 9(2), 1992, pp. 429-57.

Mediation UK, *Community Mediation Video: Mediation in the community: Training in Community Mediation Skills*, Bristol, Mediation UK, 1995.

Merry, S E, *Getting Justice and Getting Even: Legal consciousness among working-class Americans*, Chicago, University of Chicago Press, 1990.

Miller, R and Sarat, A, 'Grievances, claims and disputes: assessing the adversary culture', *Law and Society Review* 15, 1980-1.

Mulcahy, L, Selwood, M, Summerfield, L and Netton, A, *Mediation of Medical Negligence Claims: An option for the future*, London, HMSO, 2000.

Mulcahy, L and Summerfield, L, 'Keeping it in the Community: Vol. 2 – methodology report', available on request from Nuffield Foundation, 2000.

Mulcahy, L and Tritter, J, 'Pathways, pyramids and icebergs? Mapping the links between dissatisfaction and complaints', *Sociology of Health and Illness* 20(6), 1998, pp. 823-45.

Murphy, A J, 'Private correspondence with principal enforcement officer', Southwark Noise Team, 17 January 2000.

Murray, J, Rau, A S and Sherman, E F, *Processes of Dispute Resolution - The role of lawyers*, New York, Foundation Press, 1989.

Nader, L, 'Alternatives to the American judicial system' in *No Access to Law: Alternatives to the American judicial system,* L. Nader (ed.), London, Academic Press, 1980.

Odom, E, 'The mediation hearing: a primer' in *Mediation: Contexts and challenges*, Palenski and Launer (eds), 1986.

OPCS, *1991 Census: County Monitor (Inner London),* London, Office of Population, Census and Surveys, 1991.

Pavlich, G, *Justice Fragmented: Mediating community disputes under postmodern conditions,* London, Routledge, 1996.

Pavlich, G, 'The power of community mediation: government and formation of self-identity', *Law and Society Review* 30(4), 1996a, pp. 707-734.

Roberts, M, 'Who is in charge? Reflections on recent research on the role of the mediator' *Journal of Social Welfare and Family Law* 5, 1993, 372-87.

Roberts, S, 'Towards a minimal form of alternative intervention', *Mediation Quarterly* 11, 1986, 25-41.

Rothschild, J, 'Dispute transformation, the influence of a communication paradigm of disputing, and the San Francisco Community Boards Program' in *The Possibility of Popular Justice*, Merry and Milner (eds), Michigan, 1996.

Shonholtz, R, 'Neighbourhood justice systems: work, structure and guiding principles', *Mediation Quarterly* 5, 1984, pp. 3-30.

Silbey, S and Merry, S, 'Mediator Settlement Strategies', *Law and Policy* 3, 1986, pp. 7-32.

Southwark Council, http://www.southwark.gov.uk, 1999.

Southwark Mediation Centre, *1997/8 Annual Report*, London, Southwark Mediation Centre, 1998.

Southwark Mediation Centre, *1996/7 Annual Report*, London, Southwark Mediation Centre, 1997.

Southark Mediation Centre (1994) cited by M Leibmann, 'The future of community mediation', in *Achieving Civil Justice: Appropriate dispute resolution for the 1990s*, R Smith (ed.), London, Legal Action Group, 1996.

Tebay, S, Cumberbatch, G and Graham, N, *Disputes Between Neighbours,* Birmingham, Aston University, 1986.

Trubek, D, 'Studying courts in context', *Law and Society Review* 15(3-4), 1980-1, pp. 485-501.

Yngvesson, B, 'Local people, local problems and neighborhood justice: the discourse of "community" in San Francisco Community Boards', in *The Possibility of Popular Justice*, Merry and Milner (eds), Michigan, 1996.